Brave
Souls

big
ideas
library®

Brave
Souls

Find your courage, speak your truth and be happy again after sexual violence

Jennifer Potter

Published by The Big Ideas Library 2017
Copyright © Jennifer Potter, 2017
Jennifer Potter has asserted her right to be identified as the
author of this work.

First published in the United Kingdom in 2017
by The Big Ideas Library

The Big Ideas Library
20 Fountayne Street, York YO31
A CIP catalogue record for this book is available from the
British Library.
ISBN 978-0-9929859-9-8

Typeset by Ned Hoste
Printed by Inky Fingers Ltd

The Big Ideas Library is the publishing division of
The Big Ideas Collective Ltd.

Dedication

This book is dedicated to all the other Brave Souls in the world, may your heart find its' way to love x

Contents

Foreword

'Beauty begins the moment you decide to be yourself.'
Coco Chanel

This is my story. I share it with you to offer you something that I searched for twenty years to find: hope. I share it with the intention that if you, or someone you know, has also been affected by similar events, you can find your way to peace quicker than I did. I share it with you so that you know, whatever life throws at you, YOU and only YOU get to choose your life story.

I was raped when I was seventeen. After the event, I searched for twenty years for a book that would offer me hope. Hope that my life as I thought it was wouldn't be over. Hope that the dreams I had before the rape could still come true, that I could like myself again, maybe even love myself. I never found that book. I found books about suicide, books about shame, books about loss, books about half lives, books about post-traumatic stress disorder. They all seemed to be lacking in a happy ending. They were stories about how to survive, not thrive; stories about compromise.

They made me feel worse. I wanted hope. I wanted to believe a happy ending was still possible. I wanted hope that trauma doesn't lead to half a life. Hope that I could trust and, perhaps, even fall in love with a man that was worthy of my love and all I had to offer, and that I would be worthy of his love and all he had to offer me. Hope that I could live a normal life. Hope that the pain would eventually go away. Hope that the shame could be released rather than locked up (because, boy, did that take some effort). Hope that I wasn't indeed broken or damaged in the way I feared I might be. Hope that my life wasn't 'wrecked' as the media would have me believe. Hope that I could FEEL love and BE loved again.

I wanted my life back. And I was on a mission to bloody find it. I chose to thrive not just survive. Of course it wasn't always like that. There were lots of years where acceptance, compromise and half-life patterns played out. But I never gave up looking and searching.

After I was raped, I threw myself head first into my marketing career with a big corporate in the UK. I thought that was all I had left; that and my family and friendships. I believed on some level that if I could gain success through work and being a great friend, I could feel significant again, that I could make it okay. In truth I was just choosing to focus on something less painful. Over time, I became obsessed with fixing those parts of myself I believed to be broken as a result of the abuse. I studied hard, read books, went on courses, tried therapies, and all the time I was adding to my own skills both mentally and emotionally. Because of that, I am now here with a truck-load of insight, tools and tips that I want to share with other people who have been affected by sexual abuse and rape, and the families and friends trying to help them.

Of course, none of this wisdom makes me qualified or an expert on anybody else's experience. Every person's story is unique to them. Hopefully this book can offer victims some hope or, at least, a safe place to explore some ideas about what may be possible whatever part of their journey they find themselves in; to know they're not alone in how they think and feel. I don't know it all, but one thing I do know is that we all deserve to regain the happiness that gets taken from us when we are abused. We deserve to feel whole again, to feel good enough. To feel more than good enough.

So, twenty years later, after lots of learning, searching, exploring, finding, not finding, crying, shouting, screaming, achieving, breathing, being, arriving, accepting, exploring and learning some more, I'm here (phew!) writing this book for victims of sexual abuse to offer the hope I so desperately sought on my journey to thriving.

This is my journey to *thriving*, not just *surviving*.

I've been as daring as I feel able. I want you to know as much about my experience and what I've found to be helpful as possible. This requires me to bare some thoughts, feelings and experiences that, quite frankly, one part of me would much rather stay private. It makes me feel vulnerable to know people are going to have an opinion about what I've written. I offer the details of my story compassionately, as I've experienced the power that can exist in sharing your story with the right person at the right time. It gives you permission to connect on a very human level, permission to reflect, permission to be you.

I really hope that other people will find help quicker than I did. It took me twenty years to find my inner peace and I am not fully there yet. I suspect it will be an ongoing process. Twenty years of my life I spent in the rollercoaster ups and downs of emotional agony that comes with not knowing who you are anymore. I want people in need to benefit from my vast research, relentless pursuit of answers and search for happiness. Most of all I want those people to know that even though they may feel like they're in the loneliest, most helpless and hopeless of places, they are NEVER alone.

I'm a big believer that the worst of life's traumas can become a gift for us. It sounds counterintuitive, but being raped has given me many gifts. It made me hungry to learn about the human condition and choices we make, to understand empowerment, to learn compassion and empathy. It motivated me to become the coach and acupuncture therapist I am today, to be able to help others. It's made me brave beyond my expectations, it's refined my sensory acuity and it's given me this book – something I hope will help other people.

I wrote this book primarily for other women, men, girls and boys who have experienced sexual abuse. I also wrote it for their friends and families. It's a tough journey on them too, not knowing what to say to make it better or how to be around the person suffering. I hope you'll find some inspiration and a place to start or continue your journey to greater peace.

This is my story and how I changed it from surviving to thriving.

I hope it helps you or someone you love in some small but precious way.

1. The beginning of the end

'Owning our story and loving ourselves through that process is the bravest thing that we'll ever do. We must walk into the arena with courage and dare to show up.'
BRENÉ BROWN

In November 2012, with sweaty palms, a dry throat and my pensive frown, but more sure than I'd ever been, I stepped into a police station in Yorkshire to report two historical crimes. One was of sexual abuse when I was aged six and the other was rape when I was seventeen. Both incidents involved different men. Both times I knew the men. Both times I had been asleep in my bed. Both times the men had been given my parents' permission to take care of me. Both times they had been given a position of trust. Both times they had abused it.

It was nineteen years since I had been raped and twenty nine since I had been sexually abused. My intention in going to the police was only to report the incidents. I had no expectation that they would lead to a conviction; they had happened a long time ago and I knew there was no forensic evidence. The chances of going further would be slim. I was okay with that, I just wanted to do what I could to feel better about decisions I had and hadn't made. I had lived with a slippery guilt that perhaps it might have happened to someone else and that by not speaking out at the time, I could have prevented it.

For a long time, I remember thinking that I had nothing to complain about, that this was just the way it was, the way it happened to some unfortunate people. I used to think that because there were no obvious physical effects from my rape – no black eyes, bust lips and ribs, external bruising, swollen limbs – that I'd got off lightly and I therefore had nothing to complain about. I should pick myself up, dust myself down, make do and get on with life. There was a time when I felt jealous of those victims who had been violently attacked, and yes, I feel ashamed that I even had this thought. They had something I didn't, though: their pain was obvious to the outside world (at least some of it was). It was obvious to people that these victims had been through a trauma, an ordeal, because they could see it with their own eyes. You couldn't avoid it. Those people needed help, support, love.

I pretty much suffered in silence. I didn't know how to bring up how I felt a lot of the time because I couldn't articulate it and I felt ashamed, dirty, not enough. And for the rest of the time I tried like hell to pretend it had never happened. I was also worried if I spoke up I'd be found out, that people would know I wasn't as lovely as I seemed. That once people knew my dirty little secret, they would somehow judge me differently, avoid me like a disease they might catch.

So most of the time it stayed locked away.

There would come a time for me just before I stepped into the police station when the pain of holding it in outweighed the pain it might bring if I let it out. And I mean really let it out. By giving it the voice it needed, to be seen and heard for what it was: my truth, my experience, my reality.

I wanted to do what I could to put things right. I wanted to take my power back, to feel strong and safe again. On some level I wanted to see what the justice system could do to right the wrongs that had been done and prevent it from happening to someone else. And most of all I wanted *him* to know it wasn't okay what he did to me.

2. Incident 1

'Laughter is timeless, imagination has no age and dreams are forever.'
Walt Disney

Saturday nights were always fun when I was small. After my brother and I were dunked in the bath and cajoled into our night clothes, I'd usually spend some time watching my mum get ready to go out. I loved watching her dry her hair, but mostly I loved the make-up part. I can still remember the smell of her make-up bag with all its contents, a powdery perfume smell. When she'd finished painting her face, she would shimmy into her outfit, spritz some perfume behind each ear and on her wrists, and then spritz some through the air at me. She would put on her 'going out' jewellery, step into the heeled shoes I liked to totter around in when she wasn't looking and voilà, she was done, ready for a night out with my dad.

I loved watching her get ready, it was part of my 'coming of age' training, only I didn't know it back when I was six years old. It was like a glimpse into the future. You see, when I was six, all I wanted to be when I grew up was my mum. I wanted to be a wife and a mummy (and maybe a teacher) and I thought that would be enough.

On a Saturday night, my brother and I were usually allowed some treats. Typically, it involved something to eat (like Seabrook crinkle crisps or a treasured Soda Stream, kept only for the weekends) and something to watch on the TV. We liked to watch things like Dusty Bin on *3-2-1* and *Blankety Blank*, and we were usually allowed to stay up for an hour after Mum and Dad had left. Our babysitter at the time was the son of my parents' friends. He was roughly seventeen years old. When he said bedtime, we both knew it meant bedtime despite how much we rolled our eyes and moaned.

This one particular Saturday would turn out to be the last time this babysitter was allowed to sit for us. Some time into the evening, I woke up from my sleep still in my Minnie Mouse nightie. Something felt odd, I felt strange, all was not as it normally would be in my bed. I tried to move but my legs were stuck. I became aware of a wetness and a strange feeling I had never before felt between my legs. I panicked. *Had I wet the bed?* I was frozen to my bed, still unable to move. I started to panic further, but that made me freeze even more. A bang on the front door and someone jumped from the bottom of my bed and out into the corridor. It was our babysitter. *What was he doing down there?* Another bang on the front door.

I got up to get a towel from the bathroom that was next door to my bedroom for the wetness I could still feel. He was having a wee.

"What are you doing up?" he said, panic in his voice.

"I thought I'd wet the bed," I said, hanging my head in shame, taking a towel and returning to my room.

He dashed downstairs and I sat on the top step listening to him refuse my dad's offer to walk him home. I got back into bed waiting for my mum to come and check on us, like she always did.

My room was first on the landing after the bathroom and she was surprised to see me awake. I told her I thought I'd wet the bed, explained I couldn't move my legs and about the babysitter, who had appeared to be under my covers between my legs. Mostly it was all just terribly confusing. My parents gave me reassurance, tucked me back in and all was normal again. My parents were home, I was safe. I don't remember what else was said at the time, but I remember thinking it was okay now.

I've often wondered what my parents must have thought at the time. I cannot imagine what it must be like for a parent to be faced with that reality. To suspect but not know exactly what just happened to your daughter. To know the young man you had trusted to take care of your most precious treasure might have just abused that responsibility. To not know what damage and impact that might have had. To not know where to go to get help. To decide whether to have a difficult conversation with your friends or not.

In 1982 in Barnsley, where we lived at the time, people took care of their own families. Scandals were hidden, swept under the carpet. It was the passive aggressive version of mafia culture. It was the 80s, a time of 'fitting in' straight out of the period of 'keeping up with the Joneses'. Therapy was something that mad people needed and shame was a dirty word to be avoided at all costs. So my parents took the decision to limit the damage. They told the babysitter's parents that they'd decided it would be better if they had a female babysitter now that I was getting older. As for me, they decided to monitor me, keeping me close for a while to see if I seemed affected or changed by it.

Of course something had changed for me that night, but we just didn't know it at the time. How could we have? Some of my innocence was taken by that young silly teenage boy. I never went to sleep on my back from that point forward growing up and I didn't like being without underwear in bed throughout my childhood.

When I was older I would discover a weirdness around foreplay. I didn't know if it was normal, if it was good or bad. Should I enjoy it or not, was it dirty and wrong? I would freeze and try to avoid it. I would also discover this incident had affected my sense of self. I didn't feel as important. Some of my ability to feel empowered to choose for myself what I wanted rather than have things taken from me was short circuiting in my brain. It created distress and often led to submission or defensive attack.

For ten years, though, I seemed absolutely normal. In fact, I'd go so far as to say I forgot the event entirely, except for the odd inexplicable flashback. I remember one of them as if it happened yesterday. I was at primary school, probably seven or eight years old. I'd left something in my bag hanging at the end of the corridor on my allocated school peg. Having collected my missing items, I ran back down the corridor. The sun was streaming through the high windows making square patterns on the floor reflecting the window frames. There was a calmness to the moment, all felt just as it should. Then the memory came like a movie flashing out in front of me – the wet feeling, the man under the covers, the unusual sensation in my body. It halted my run. *What is that?* That same feeling again, that something wasn't right. And as fast as it came back it me, it ran away and I ran to class. Forgotten again.

It wasn't until I was raped, aged seventeen, that the whole event finally came flooding back to me, sat in a doctor's surgery sobbing.

3. Incident 2

'What hurts you blesses you. Darkness is your candle'
Rumi

One summer's evening, my parents, my aunty and I had gone to a family BBQ in Barnsley, South Yorkshire. My dad and his two sisters came from a large family. My grandma had been one of nine siblings and many of them had large families themselves. There were a lot of cousins.

One of my dad's cousins, the middle of three boys, married with two young children and in his early 30s, took a particular interest in me. He was at the BBQ with his then wife. She was sassy and I admired her a lot. I admired him too. He had a larger than life confidence. I would later come to know very clearly the difference between confidence and arrogance.

He would tap my bum as he passed and throw me a wink, which I thought was quite forward, but then noticed him doing it to other women. I assumed it was his way and I didn't think I was in any way being singled out, although I was flattered by his attention. In a group conversation, he invited me out with him and his wife and their friends, offering to show me around town for a night out. I was seventeen at the time. He asked my dad for permission and Dad replied, 'It's up to her, she's her own woman, but if she does, you make sure you look after her'.

My dad was pretty passionate about me being independent. He wanted me to earn my own money so I wouldn't have to be dependent on a man. If my car ever needed any work, he insisted I watched while he taught me how to fix the problem (much to my frustration). I didn't know many girls my age who could check the oil, change a tyre and knew how to check and clean the spark plugs. I was also his precious treasure, his little girl and he wanted me to be happy.

Phone numbers were swapped and two weeks later I was driving over to their home for a night out in Barnsley. I wore beige jeans and a wool sleeveless top. The night passed without incident, at least not anything obvious to me.

I drank lager half pints and sometimes missed a round. There was talk about me being single and that the 'right one would turn up'. We drank until last orders then got a taxi home to their house. I was sleeping on their sofa. At around 4am, as he got up to go to work in the mines of North Yorkshire, he stroked my hand that was hanging off the sofa to wake me. He told me he was pleased I'd come over and gone out with him and his friends. He invited me out for his birthday, which was two weeks away, and told me it wouldn't be the same if I wasn't there. Then he kissed me, a peck, half on my lips half my cheek. It felt wrong. I figured he must have been confused, sleepy or still drunk, or perhaps I'd misread something.

When I returned to my aunty's house where I was staying for the summer holiday, I told her I'd had an okay night, that he'd invited me out for his birthday and that I wasn't sure if I wanted to go.

She said, 'Don't go then'.

Like it was simple. It didn't feel simple to me. It felt like I'd be letting them down. I wasn't very good at saying no and I felt bound by his persuasion. I had learnt to become a people pleaser, not someone who 'upset the apple cart'.

I would later be told by my contact at the charity IDAS, who support victims of abuse in Yorkshire, that his behaviour was typical of grooming. I feel naïve now even writing this. Why didn't I just make up an excuse or say no? Why was that so difficult for me? I was flattered by his attention. I had never experienced attention from an older man like that. I wasn't the most confident girl, certainly not about the way I looked and the opposite sex.

The night arrived and I decided to go at the last minute. I hadn't been able to think of a way to not go, an excuse, a suitable lie. There was an unwritten rule about families and sticking together and I felt wrapped up in that obligation somehow.

I wore a floor-length wraparound skirt, which was fashionable at the time, it was blue and white checked, and a blue vest top. There was a bigger group this time and we went from pub to pub through town. We were all drinking, for me mainly lager halves again and later a couple of bottles of K cider.

I don't remember feeling drunk. He did the same flirting, bum patting, trying to dance with everyone including me. Then we went to a nightclub. There was some dancing, he dragged me to the dance floor and started dancing with me. I remember it feeling too intimate, too close to me, so I went to the toilet. I remember feeling uncomfortable. In the toilet I bumped into my oldest friend who I'd grown up with. I told her I felt uncomfortable and didn't want to go back with them. My instinct was kicking in. She offered for me to stay at hers and collect my stuff in the morning. Another occasion of not knowing how to let people down. I felt unable to say yes, worrying what the 'family' would think of me. It would be a sliding doors moment. If only I'd said yes.

We left to go home in a taxi and I went straight to bed. I was sleeping in one of their son's bedrooms this time. The boys were staying with their grandma. It was hot in the room, so with the window open I slept in my vest top and pants on top of the sheets on the single bed.

Some time into the night, he entered my room, wrapped in only his dark blue dressing gown. He tried to kiss me, I pushed him away. He kept telling me how much he liked me, that he wanted me. I told him to leave, to go back to his bed, but he wouldn't listen. I tried to reason with him. I told him he was drunk, that he was making a mistake. I begged him. From there, it escalated until he threw off his dressing gown while pinning me to the bed still trying to kiss me. I moved my head away still trying to reason with him, 'Your wife is next door, please stop. This is your son's bed, please stop. I don't want this, please stop.' He moved a hand to my pants and we battled, he to get them off and I to keep them on.

I had only one hand on my pants, the other was trying to push him off. I pleaded for him to stop, to return to his wife next door, to leave me alone. I begged him. I lost the battle of the pants, they were whipped from my hand with what seemed like no effort at all to him. Exposed, vulnerable and backed up against the wall with nowhere to run, I pleaded with him that I was saving my virginity and to please stop, one, more, time.

In what seemed like a flash, he was on top of me, my legs forced open and inside me. It was too late.

All I can remember at that moment was freezing and turning my head away toward the wall unable to fight back his heavy body, the pain between my legs, my voice unable to speak. I was mute. It was like life had stopped. I had stopped breathing. I had stopped living.

And at some point 'it' stopped.

He rolled off to the wall and I slid onto the floor collecting my clothes heading straight to the bathroom to hide. I said nothing. Locking the door, I took the soap and rubbed it over my face, in my mouth, between my legs, trying to clean myself. I felt dirty. I felt shame. I felt panic. I sat on the toilet lid for what seemed like forever, shaking, waiting. I looked at the bathroom floor, my life shattered across it. I tried to sweep up the broken pieces, desperately working out what this now meant and what I should do. It would be at this point of reflection that the strategy 'damage limitation' was decided.

I tried to put myself in his wife's shoes, I felt ashamed and guilty, like I had done something wrong. I thought about his two young boys and imagined their lives knowing their dad was 'one of those'. I thought of his mum and dad and the shame they'd experience in the family. I thought of my mum and saw how their dreams for me finding a good man, one who would love me, were now also shattered on this bathroom floor. I thought about my dad, about how I had always been so precious to him and now I'd let him down in the worst possible way. The weight of shame got heavier and heavier until the curtain came down.

Damage limitation: do nothing, say nothing.

As the dark started to turn to light, I left the comfort of the bathroom. He had returned to his bed. As soon as it was light enough, I grabbed my things, left a note and got into my car. The note said something like 'Thank you for inviting me out and for having me to stay. I had a hangover and couldn't sleep so I left.' It seems ridiculous to me now that I would have even written this note, and I can also see how it was my way of trying to escape out of the back door without drama, to ignore what had just happened to me and its ripple effect on the people around me.

It was too early to return to my aunty's without her knowing something was wrong, so I drove to a road near her house, pulled over and waited some more. I didn't want to talk about it, I didn't want to acknowledge what it was, what had just happened to me. I knew it was wrong and I didn't feel the same. I felt dirty. Shamed. Life would never be the same again. I'd already made my decision: no sharing. Damage limitation.

When I thought it was a reasonable time to go home to my aunty's, I started the car again. It was still early and I had to wake my aunty to let me in. I didn't want her to look at me, so I looked at the floor and asked if I could go shower, faking a hangover face. As I shed my clothes and crept into the shower to attempt to scrub my body clean of the disgust, I silently sobbed my shock and shame down the plug hole. My aunty would later tell me, around the time of the court case, that she'd thought I was acting out of character when I returned home so early, but had assumed I was suffering from the hangover I had claimed. And that would be that.

In the following week I disclosed to two friends what had happened. I still didn't want to give it the 'rape' label, despite one of my friends telling me that's what it was and the other encouraging me to go to the police. It was just too overwhelming for me at the time. I told them to tell no one.

Some few weeks later, I was stood in a larger group of friends at college in the breakout areas, and one happened to mention a rape case that had hit the news. There was a comment about 70% of rapes being by someone you knew, someone in your family, and I felt a few eyes staring at me more intently. I wasn't sure if they knew, if they'd been told, but the shame-o-meter certainly kicked in again and I wanted to hide some more. It reinforced my shame and drove another nail in the box that was never to be opened again.

I wish I'd listened to my instinct. I had two opportunities to listen to my intuition which had told me loud and clear 'You are not safe with this person'. I wish I'd been able to say no more easily without worrying about upsetting people's feelings. I wish I'd learnt that to say no is okay and you don't need an excuse or a lie either. Your life is your life and you have to live it, even if it means potentially upsetting someone else.

I am bound by frustration into a soul of another.
One I cannot understand
One I cannot free myself from
She toils by night
In a world of semi consciousness
Evaporating her strength into the raping night
By day she fights hard to hold back her watery sadness
Without the knowledge she needs to show the world
how much she hurts

So bad it rips at her insides
Separating her personalities
into two war parties
Tangling among her insides
Cannonballing her heart and blowing up her brain
in the endless battle
to find out whether she is a victory winner
or a pacifist
She knows deep inside that she is
rock solid
outside
and that she can find the secret inside
to let go
of the demons
that haunt her tainted mind
But she knows she can only do this alone
And only she knows where that special key is embedded
To unlock her past and set her free
(J Potter, age 18, shortly after being raped)

4. Not telling the police

'You've always had the power my dear, you just had to learn it for yourself.'
Glenda, Wizard of Oz

It was 1995 when I was raped. I was 17 and just about to head off to university. At the time, I could think of nothing more terrifying than telling the police. Back then, the papers reported female victims of rape being strung out in court like dirty linen, picking at any and every hole in their character, finding a way to prove that they were 'asking for it': a skirt the wrong length; too much flesh; the wrong colour lipstick. All signs that you'd brought this on yourself.

It was my final year at college and I was just about to embark on my A level exams. Life at this age was hard enough; you're not a child anymore and you're not quite a fully matured adult either. You're in no man's land, trying to work out who you are outside what your parents and friends have taught you. I was a fairly likeable girl at seventeen and had lots of friends, but certainly my insecurities were starting to show up (as they do at this age).

I'd had one boyfriend. We'd snogged by the sports hall and in my bedroom. Other than that I was pretty inexperienced. College was all about fitting in or being different and cool. I was opting for option one – fit in – with any leftover energy put into option two – be cool. I didn't need a scandal on my hands nor did I need to deal with the shame of being raped whilst getting through my A-Levels: damage limitation.

The problem with being a people person is that you're constantly putting other people's needs first. This is something I'd done all my life. It felt nice to be acknowledged for doing something good.

I started to rationalise. Only the two of us knew, and only I had been hurt as far as I could assess. To speak out equalled more hideous experiences for me and a whole lot of drama and more pain for everyone else close to me (and to him). And what of his poor family? I remember thinking, two kids, a wife, parents, brothers, their families ... Oh it went on until it spiralled so that the responsibility for everyone else felt so overwhelming I stuck to my initial strategy: damage limitation.

I blamed myself. I remember thinking it must have been my fault. Bad things like this couldn't have happened to me unless I'd said or done the wrong thing. I'd been a virgin at the time and a very naïve seventeen-year-old. I don't mind confessing the thought of sex terrified me. I had no idea how the whole sex thing worked beyond making a baby and outside of my hopes for a proper boyfriend my age. I was saving myself, as per my mum's advice. I thought if I was friendly, grew to know someone, hung out with them for a while, we'd probably have a conversation about 'going out' and from there we'd have more conversations as we decided to try other things. I was hoping for a Prince Charming, a love I could be swept away with.

After being raped, I couldn't imagine how anyone would want to go anywhere near me. Surely this meant I was now damaged goods.

So with all those things combined – the current public perception of rape victims (that they weren't indeed victims at all), my age and what was happening in my life at the time, my need to be liked, my people-pleaser mentality, the shame and the blame, the horror and the pain – my mind was made up. There was no way I was going to the police: damage limitation.

And so it was.

A few weeks after the incident, I became aware of a searing pain in my groin area which didn't feel like anything menstrual related. My mum made me go to the doctors as it was getting worse. It felt like the energy of the physical trauma was still trapped in my body, in its most delicate part.

After an intense session with my 'matter of fact' doctor, who grilled me on my sexual experience, I felt unable to contain it. Such was the shame, I tried to avoid telling her the whole truth. I told her that I hadn't wanted to do 'it', that I had been forced outside a nightclub. I also told her that I didn't know the man who did it. The truth was I have always been pretty crap at lying and I couldn't bear more shame from the lies, so I eventually told the doctor everything, the whole truth, breaking my silence and breaking down in tears with the release.

In the moment of sharing, I felt a sense of relief, so much so that I heard myself saying, 'This isn't the first time I've been abused'. *This was new news to me. Had it happened before?* As I sat there unravelling the details of the rape, I had uncovered an earlier memory from when I was aged six, and it was as clear to me as if it happened yesterday: I had been abused by a babysitter.

I know now that it's very common for memories to be temporarily hidden, particularly if there is great emotion, trauma or, in my case, bewilderment around the experience. My brain didn't know where to store it, so it didn't. It left it out there in the ether. But now I did know what it was and I could store it in its appropriate place in my brain, but I was already dealing with a lot. The doctor would strongly encourage me to tell my mum and dad. She sent me away, to return with my parents later in the week to discuss what next.

As I reached home, my eyes swollen and red, my mum waited in the kitchen preparing dinner like a normal evening in our home. Lord knows what she must have thought, but she could see I had been crying. There was no hiding anymore.

"What's the matter, what did the doctor say?" she said.

I was stood in the middle of the second worst experience of my life, I felt frozen to the spot in the kitchen, like another fridge. Lifeless, I stared at her, unable to look anywhere else, my bottom lip trembling and eyes searing from the pokey tears about to push themselves out.

I think I was hoping I could tell her telepathically, like it would make it easier if I didn't need to say it, to say 'that' word. After what felt like forever, quivering and crying out spewed three words, 'I've been raped'.

To begin with my Mum couldn't take it in and she just stood looking at me, mouth hanging open. She was in shock. Words she hoped she'd never have to hear. Five minutes before she'd been cooking dinner for us all, and now this.

'What did you say?' came her reply.

'I've been raped.'

She stood looking at me, staring at me. She still couldn't take it in.

'What do you mean? By who?'

'It happened when I stayed in Barnsley, Dad's cousin.'

'I can't take this in,' she said. And as she stood in her own shock and trauma she knew only one thing, that she needed her wing-man, she needed her husband. 'I need your dad,' she said, and off she went to the garage to fetch him.

I stood in the kitchen, alone. The story I was telling myself at the time was that she hadn't believed me, that she thought I was being a drama queen, attention seeking. And now she'd gone to get Dad I was in serious trouble. I wasn't afraid of my dad, but he was always threatened if either me or my brother were really naughty growing up, the 'Just wait 'til I tell your dad' kind of threat.

At that moment in the kitchen, I knew he would explode (as any father would), but I wasn't ready for it, the drama, the shock, the anger, everyone else's emotions filling up the space of the house. I was still coming to terms with my honesty in revealing the truth to the doctor, let alone thinking about my own feelings, and here I was receiving everyone else's emotions and the chain reactions.

It wasn't the explosion I feared the most though, it was the loss of his love for me. The shame I felt that I wouldn't be his precious daughter anymore. Would he still love me if he knew this about me, how I'd let him down, how I wasn't precious anymore?

I stood in the kitchen alone as Mum entered the door to the garage where Dad was with my brother. The rest of that evening is like a weird movie in my mind, where you see the highlights but in slow motion.

There was rage, talk of going to 'his' house with a rifle he used for game keeping and 'sorting' it. There was lots of shouting, some hugs, lots of discussion, my brother in the background, more tears, my tears, their tears, me still stood frozen to the kitchen floor. Then some calmness and a more rational conversation: they needed more information.

'Tell us exactly what happened,' my dad said. I told him the surface level details.

It was decided they'd ring 'his' father, my dad's uncle.

I don't remember the conversation, but I can still see my dad standing in the hallway where our telephone sat atop a fixed wall unit and mirror, phone pushed to the side of his head. I learned later that my dad had been asked if he believed me. 'Why wouldn't I?' he said. 'She's standing in tears in my kitchen, shaking.'

My dad was told to leave it with his uncle to sort. Later that night, we received another phone call this time from my rapist, the cousin. He denied it all. He said he was too drunk to have done anything and woke on the sofa in the early hours of the morning. I don't remember much else about that evening other than crying in my room alone. I was making friends with my shame. It would become a loyal but unwanted friendship.

What I didn't realise at the time was that in that moment, that evening, I would choose on some subconscious level to shut myself off from love, because I didn't think I deserved it anymore. I had decided I was unlovable.

I'd shamed my parents and our family name, it must have been my fault. I was now becoming a hindrance to the family. I would spend many a year wondering if my parents loved me or not. The truth was that they surrounded me with love all the time, it was always there, I just didn't know how to let it in after being raped because I felt ashamed. I believed I had allowed one of the most precious things

I had to offer another human being to be taken from me. So now I wasn't precious anymore.

A few days later my parents and I returned to the doctors. Counselling support and the police were offered up as solutions. For most of the time, I sat looking at the floor, mute. This was my second chance to tell the police and I declined for all the same reasons as before, only now I was also dealing with my parents' reaction to it. Shock and fury had been the big themes alongside helplessness, not knowing what to do or say to make it better for me. My parents thought I should go to the police, especially my dad. He wanted him to pay for his crime. Truth is I was petrified, overwhelmed and deeply hurting on the inside. It was all I could do to put one foot in front of the other. My parents made sure I knew that it would be my decision and they'd stand beside me whatever I decided. Damage limitation remained ...

The shock and fury was out there in the space between us and the shame levels rocketed now there were people whom I loved, who knew I was ruined and damaged. *Would they still love me back?* I would retreat even further into my loneliness. So I tried to make it all go away by putting it into a box. The lid was nailed on tight and it was swept under the carpet, under the bed, superglued in.

Life went on.

5. Telling the police

'Learn the alchemy true human beings know. The moment you accept what troubles you've been given, the door will open.'

Rumi

It was now 2012 and the time had arrived when my need to tell the police became greater than the fears or beliefs I had about not telling them. It was nineteen years since the rape and twenty nine years after the first sexual attack.

In that twenty years we'd managed mainly to avoid 'that' part of the family. My family lived in York, I had run away to Berkshire for my career and they still lived in Barnsley. We visited other closer family in Barnsley and some of them came to visit us, but mainly we stayed away from the wider family events. My parents attended one or two funerals that his parents also attended, but no words were shared. It was a family-kept secret.

In that time, a few things had happened in my life, almost like the universe was conspiring to move me to speaking my truth. I'd been having acupuncture, which was propelling me forward in my healing both physically and emotionally. I took voluntary redundancy from my corporate job in a technology business to follow my dreams of running my own business. And I moved back home to Yorkshire having lived away for fifteen years. I was at my strongest. I felt more empowered and in charge of my life than I ever had before. I was following my dreams to run my own business, answering a call from my heart to move home to a city I loved and to be near my family. I truly felt liberated.

And something else HUGE was happening in the UK at the time. The explosion of the Jimmy Saville scandal had just happened. It was everywhere. It blew up in everyone's faces. You couldn't avoid it. Jimmy Saville was a famous broadcaster and TV presenter in the UK who had used his privileged position to abuse and rape children. The abuse had been covered over for years, decades even, because of his popularity and connection with people of power. Disgusting and unacceptable behaviour that went on for years and with some of our most vulnerable individuals. A total disgrace.

Finally the UK had to listen because some investigative journalists didn't give up trying to tell the story that needed to be told. I stood on the sidelines, watching curiously. The world seemed different, the scales of justice starting to balance out with more thought toward the care of the victims. How can we protect these people? What did we do wrong? How can we do it better? How can we make sure this never happens again? Victims started stepping out, wanting to finally be rid of their story, to share, to offload, to seek the justice they'd always deserved. And I felt enraged on their behalf but curious. The world seemed different; people were paying attention, things were changing for the better and I was stronger.

In a cherished father-daughter moment, I told my dad I was thinking about doing something to help others who'd been abused or raped, maybe share my story, offer some coaching tools I'd found helpful in a book or workshop. I'd been sharing some of my coaching tools with him to help with his golf that day. I was feeling very grateful that I had such loving and supportive parents. This was the first time we'd spoken directly about what happened since the events in the doctor's room.

Then I said it ...

'Do you think I should have told the police?'

'Yes, absolutely. What he did to you was wrong and he should be made to pay.'

And there it was in the room: the evidence that my parents believed me. Clarity. As simple as that, and I knew what I had to do.

I think, looking back, I had already decided, I just wanted to hear I had their support, and with my dad behind me I felt it was possible.

One wintery day in November 2012, I happened to be driving past the local police station and, as if on autopilot, I turned into the car park and walked into the reception. I was shaking, I felt like I was on stage without a script, naked. The police reception was just how it looks on TV in *The Bill* or *Eastenders*, an unloved area, lacking in personality. I remember blue plastic chairs bolted to the floor, grey walls, a funny dusty sterile smell. There was one other person sat in the waiting room and a policeman sat protected behind a glass counter, reading paperwork. I approached the counter, trembling, dry throat again, feeling like a child, a nuisance.

'I'm here to report a historical crime,' I said

The policeman on the desk didn't hear me clearly the first time and asked me to repeat it again. I had probably mumbled in my desire to get it out quick so I couldn't change my mind. I started to sweat, my breathing increased, I felt very, very small all of a sudden. The policeman just stared at me, emotionless. I felt like I was having an out of body experience. Perhaps I even felt seventeen again.

'I'm here to report a historical crime,' I said

He nodded. 'Please take a seat. Someone will come and speak to you shortly.'

The rest of this part in the process was relatively easy. I was taken to a small room and asked to provide more details. I was reporting two crimes: one when I was six years old and woke to find my male seventeen-year-old babysitter abusing me, and the other when I was seventeen and was raped by a distant family member who was supposed to be looking after me.

That was that. An officer would get in touch to take a full statement, I was told.

I left. And life continued. It was all a bit surreal. I'd taken the first step. The hardest part was done, or so I thought.

A week or two later a young female officer came to my home to take my full witness statement. It took over four hours and two full reporting books. North Yorkshire is one of the few counties who didn't at the time offer video interviews, which meant if this went to court, I would have to attend to undergo cross-examination in person. I hadn't been prepared for the level of detail they would ask in the witness statement. For example, 'When you say you had one hand holding on to your pants, which hand was it? Can you remember?' It was twenty years ago and I was right back there in that small bedroom and I was petrified again.

The detail of the evidence in the witness statement is important because that's the only thing the barristers have to work with if the case gets to court, unless there is forensic evidence. Facts, not feelings.

Facts. It's your word against theirs at the end of the day, so the more information the police have, the better. Of course, you can only remember what you can remember and that is also fine, especially with historical crimes. The young police woman was really sweet and gave me time to cry when I needed to (although by this point I had spent twenty years practising the art of holding those little buggers in if I needed to, so was pretty good at staying choked up). Learning to cry again would be something that came from therapy. I noticed the tension in my body, a familiar feeling.

I was on my own when I gave my statement, thinking it might have been upsetting or weird for my mum or dad to be sat with me hearing it all in its full gory detail. I wish now that I'd asked a friend to sit with me, or at least sit in the next room for when it was over. I was exhausted, physically and emotionally.

It was very upsetting having to relive it all in such detail. It brought it all back to me, but I was seeing it in detail through grown-up eyes, not those of a vulnerable seventeen-year-old. It made me really angry. In fact, I felt furious. What had he been thinking? How dare he! You poor child.

After giving my statement, I was asked two questions that are standard questions for witness statements:

1. Are you happy for the police to pass this case to the CPS (Crown Prosecution Service) if they think there's enough evidence to prosecute?

2. Are you willing to give evidence in court if CPS decide there is a strong case for conviction?

Another part of me spoke up: 'Yes!' and 'Yes!'

Woah, where did that come from?

Some other part of me seemed to be speaking. It was the empowered grown-up in me that had seen the event through new eyes, saw the injustice, saw all the pain I'd suffered, and wanted to make it right again. Well, as right as it could ever be, I thought.

A few weeks later, I went through it all again for my official statement. Another six hours of detailed note-taking. I was emotionally shattered again. I was told that although there wasn't forensic evidence, there was a lot of other evidence, which put the case in a good light for being taken forward including:

- I had told my parents about the abuse aged six.
- I had told my doctor not long after the rape aged seventeen, and subsequently my parents, which meant it would be logged in my medical records.
- There had been a phone call between my dad and his dad.
- I had told two friends at the time.
- I had been for various therapy over the years to try and work things out.

Most of those individuals were willing to step forward and provide a witness statement to that effect; another thing I am very grateful for.

I had not expected it to get this far. I had assumed that since it was so long ago and there was no forensic evidence, it would only go so far as investigation. I had prepared myself that the best that would happen for my justice would be that he'd be interviewed by a police person and feel told off. I would have to accept that was all that would be done. And yet here I was being told there was a good chance the rape incident would get put forward to the CPS. It was a significant moment for me in the journey, another demonstration of feeling understood, heard, acknowledged.

It was around this time I was assigned a support person from IDAS, a charity that provides comprehensive support services to individuals affected by domestic abuse and sexual violence. I didn't see my first support person much as I didn't feel I needed to; I was feeling strong. She moved to another region not long afterwards and I was then assigned another lovely lady who would be alongside me on my journey from that point onwards. I have been very grateful for her wisdom and support, particularly around the court appearance that would follow, and I now consider her a kindred spirit too.

Reporting the crime to the police was one of the hardest and the easiest things I've ever chosen to do. Easy because it's the right thing, hard because I sensed it would no longer be in my control. Men and women should not be allowed to think they can abuse another human being and get away with it. It's wrong. Full stop. The end.

There are no shades of justice here either: it's black and white, right or wrong. Of course there are parts of the justice system still to catch up. When there is no forensic evidence, any case will come down to you versus them, and as such the defence are still allowed to use whatever they can to try and discredit you as a victim and witness. It should make no difference whether you've made mistakes along the way (haven't we all?), whether you work in the sex industry, whether you went on to be promiscuous (a known and well researched effect of being sexually abused, as victims typically lose a lot if not all of their self-worth). The odds of living a normal life after the effects of such trauma aren't exactly stacked in favour of the victim, let's be honest here.

Four months after reporting it to the police, I had a total meltdown.

6. The Meltdown

'There is no passion to be found in settling for a life that is less than the one you are capable of living.'
Nelson Mandela

It was 2013 and I was trying to build my new business, I was studying every weekend, trying to settle into my new home and make new friends. On top of all this, I'd opened Pandora's box in my therapy sessions in the middle of the police investigation. I felt totally out of control, totally unsupported, like I was trying to operate my life without firm ground to stand on.

Which, of course, is irrational because I was actually surrounded by fantastic parents, great friends and making wonderful new friends too, but I felt alone within myself. I was suddenly frightened again, afraid for my safety at home, having panic attacks when going to bed, unable to settle into sleep, worried someone would attack me. My self-esteem was hanging on by a thread and I was struggling to know what to do that would be helpful. I didn't feel in control anymore.

I felt like I'd thrown a bag of marbles into the air (my life) and was standing marbleless, waiting to see where they'd all land, without any control of the process or end result. The part of me that was resourceful and independent felt like it was falling off a cliff without a parachute and no landing opportunity in sight. I felt helpless and hopeless again, just how I'd felt when I was raped.

I was usually in fix-it mode. It was one of my modus operandi, a default position, a survival strategy I was well trained in. I needed to do something, take action, make it all okay. I needed to avoid the pain that was surfacing. At the time, I was mainly living off my savings because my business was new and spare cash was limited, but I made the decision to find my own therapist and get stuck in. It was a decision I would not regret.

I had been reading Brené Brown's *Daring Greatly*, which I recommend to everyone. It's a life-changing book. It would be her wisdom from this book and gentle persuasion from my old acupuncturist which finally inspired me to find a good therapist and commit to my own healing. I had really resisted this part of the process for years, wanting to find the elusive quick fix in order to thrive, not just survive. But, sadly, there wasn't one. My brain would play tricks on me and tell me I'd done enough, that I was fixed after a short burst of some therapy, and for some time I would feel better. But I was never thriving. I was peeling off the onion layers for sure, but mainly I was only collecting the dry outer ones which were peeling off on their own. I was never digging deep into the fresh healthy flesh.

I discovered quick fixes were actually sabotaging my efforts by trying to keep me from addressing the really painful stuff, and that's EXACTLY where I needed to go.

Funny how things work out sometimes. I decided I wanted a

strong female therapist, someone who would jump in with me, help me understand, help me grow, challenge me when my ego got in the way, support me and guide me. In hindsight I was searching for a motherly nurturing connection, someone who might be able to relate to my physical and emotional pain.

I searched the local therapist website and connected with one specific woman and her photo, I don't know why. She looked formidable. I called her, she was fully booked. Damn! I found another woman and went for an initial meeting. She wasn't right. She wasn't formidable enough. I decided to approach the NHS to see what support was available to me.

A few weeks of waiting and I was sent for an assessment for both therapy and counselling. Sadly, my overall experience was pretty disappointing with the NHS and I hope they have now improved things for people like me. The therapy assessment came first. I was asked to complete a form to assess how much I warranted support from the NHS. I was still trying to hang on to the idea that I was okay, that this would pass, and although I knew how I really felt deep down, my head didn't want to be honest, to accept it was as bad as it was, so I didn't tell the whole truth on the form. I didn't tick the box that said I'd thought about suicide. I felt ashamed. It wasn't that I wanted to die, I just didn't know how to live. The part of me that didn't like helpless and hopeless could see no other option.

So I lied. I was told by the assessor that because I hadn't declared myself a risk to myself or others on the questionnaire, I didn't warrant any therapy courtesy of the NHS. In fact, their assessment of me was that I seemed to just have a lot on. With setting up a new business, moving home and now the police investigation, no wonder I was feeling frazzled. Perhaps counselling could help me feel more supported?

I had tentatively completed the questionnaire hovering over those questions, contemplating was I suicidal? Had I ever thought about actually doing it? The honest answer was no, not actually doing it. However, I had thought about how I might if I ever hit one of those really low points again, and that was what this was starting to feel like. I was in hopeless and helpless territory but without the stability of a regular salary I had been used to, creating even more instability.

Before I left, the therapist told me I should be aware of current NHS guidelines on supporting individuals who are going through a police investigation with the possibility of a court appearance. Because of these guidelines, it would be difficult for me to have support from the NHS because NHS therapists have to take lots of notes, and should my case get to court, the court could request the notes, which could be used by the defence against me to discredit me as a witness, to relay to the jury how unhinged I am, perhaps. Of course it's all speculation, but it would make an open, honest conversation more difficult.

What? I sat staring at her. This all seemed so backwards. Hang on, I thought, what about what I needed? What about how I was feeling?

Regardless of the investigation, I needed help. It felt like the NHS were covering their back, not mine (which I know is not the case). A big part of that guideline is to protect the integrity of the court case. But it made me angry. The person who needs care and support should be the priority, and whatever gets discussed should be confidential between the patient and the therapist. End of. This is not need-to-know information and, after all, if it did get to court, I am not the one on trial. This is one policy that should be changed in my opinion.

A few weeks later, still clinging on, I went to meet the NHS counsellor. She started by telling me she'd met with the therapist who assessed me and they had discussed my case. This didn't feel nice. *How dare they discuss me without my permission.* The counsellor was really nice and she tried to help me. She really did. She recounted the issue about NHS notes and evidence.

'I want to try and support you as best I can, and our only way around it would mean that we couldn't talk about the elephant in the room,' she said.

This meant that not only would we not be able to talk about the rape, but any notes taken could be used in court as evidence. So, better not to say anything.

What a waste of f***king time. I was really angry this time. I felt let down. Unsupported. The opposite of what I had been looking for. I knew this woman was desperately trying to offer me support as best she could within their systems framework, but it wasn't enough. Hopeless and helpless again and very f**king angry. How could any of that be helpful for me? What about me and my needs? I left in tears. I did try one or two sessions, but the frustration of not being able to show up fully was getting in the way of what I really needed.

I felt alone and isolated in my pain. I had reached out to professionals for support, which was not something I found easy. Something (that other voice again?) told me to look up the formidable therapist, try her again, maybe she now had a vacant slot. So I called her, and she had availability. I truly believe that I was always meant to have therapy with my formidable therapist. She would turn out to be a truly significant part of my journey and I shall be grateful to her for the rest of my life.

With the gentle and sometimes challenging support of my new

therapist, I learnt to connect with the pain, make friends with it, accept it as part of who I am and that it will gradually heal. If you've been through what I've been through, I would definitely recommend finding a good gestalt therapist. It was really powerful for me in my journey to healing. In fact, I think everyone should have a therapist at some point in their life, preferably sooner rather than later. It helps you explore who you are, how you've been shaped by life and what it all means to you now.

I was of course still looking for my quick fix, thinking two months of weekly sessions would do it. We agreed to commit to a weekly program of six weeks. If it was helping, we'd reassess at the end whether another six sessions were required. *Great, someone who talks my language.* So I ended up committing to lots of quick fix bursts which added up to a journey of discovery that would last over two years, so you could say long-term. Ironic, right?

There were several times along the way when a voice in my head would say, 'That's enough now, I think we're done here' and I would take a break or suggest slowing down or stopping. I'd end up going back for more, of course, as another part of me knew that at those points we were usually just getting to the nitty gritty and I was fearful. I was genuinely frightened and scared that I wouldn't know myself at the end. I remember thinking, what if I change so significantly that I don't know who I am or, worse still, what if I dislike myself? Thankfully, therapy wasn't like that for me. It helped me to connect to the person I already was, to accept all of me, even the bits I didn't like or denied about myself, like the angry me, the judgemental me, the sanctimonious me, the critical me.

It's time to banish the stigma attached to therapy. It's useful for all of us regardless of what journey we've been on. It's not only something for mad or broken people anymore. We should embrace it wholeheartedly. It helps you show up in life as the version of you that you were always meant to be, not the version you think you should be.

What I now know to be true is that I couldn't have got through court and the life that was happening around it without my therapist's support, guidance and wisdom. She held a space for me that no other person in my life would have been able to hold in order for me to heal, that I will treasure for the rest of my life.

7. Insights from the therapy sofa

'We delight in the beauty of the butterfly, but rarely admit the changes it has gone through to achieve that beauty.'

MAYA ANGELOU

My journey through therapy has been rich and varied, like an Indiana Jones adventure full of challenge, mystery, monsters, adversaries, champions, highs, lows and ultimate victory.

I was frightened to begin with that as we peeled back the layers I would turn into someone else, a someone else I didn't like very much. That I might find out things I didn't like about me and then I'd really not be able to live with myself. There were also times I wanted to throw in the towel, to stop. I'd had enough because it was tough. It's like looking in the mirror of your inner life and then putting a microscope on your outer life. It's intense at times, painful, emotional, annoying even, and also liberating, peaceful, curious, healing and hopeful.

Several times I heard a voice in my head saying, 'You're fixed. You can stop now.' Of course I wasn't, it was the part of me that was tired, that wanted to stay the way I was, because it was safe there. Thankfully another part of me (and a gentle nod from some wonderful guardian angels in my life) made me stay for the long haul.

The following excerpts are insights from my journal that provide a flavour of some of my intrepid journey through therapy. I had been used to keeping a journal before as a useful way of reflecting. It helped me to make sense of my experience and my later reflections, which deepened the journey of healing for me.

Session 9

It's tough.

Still.

So much progress made.

Still so far to go.

Weary explorer.

Hungry and thirsty.

But tiredness keeps winning.

Themes which seem to be showing up for me are:

- Not feeling good enough.
- Surviving because that's what I've always done (not thriving).
- Not feeling worthy/having self-worth.
- Rage and fury for one man's selfish actions wrecking so much of my life (lack of forgiveness).
- Grief for the things I'll never have, such as a normal virginity experience.
- Grief for the relationships I threw away because I didn't think I deserved them.
- Being a bloody people pleaser and not putting my needs first.
- Keeping so busy so I don't have to feel the pain or face what

needs to be faced.
- Not letting go and meeting despair head on.

Therapy is helping. I've noticed subtle differences in everyday choices I'm making. Those decisions seemed to be coming subconsciously, not consciously, which is curious for me. This is a big move forward. Some things are still a battle between head and heart, though. My body seems to know what it needs but so often my head gets in the way. I keep thinking about Martha Beck's book, *Finding your North Star* and her concept of Social Self vs Essential Self. Social Self is that part of you that plays out all the should – ought to's, in other words – what other people have told you is the 'right' thing to do, so you 'fit in'. Your Essential Self doesn't give a toss about that if it knows it's true for you and who you were always meant to be. I feel like my Social Self is ruling; I'm being guided by what I think I SHOULD do, rather than what I WANT to do. I think it's fear. It thinks it's keeping me safe if I play small, if I comply.

But safe from what?

Being hurt?

Trapped?

Being miserable?

Not being loved because of it?

Sticking my head above the parapet?

I'm learning my needs are important and that I should always ask, 'What do I want?' and 'What serves me best?' But it's still sometimes a battle with my fear of offending others if I say no, fear of not being liked, fear of not fitting someone else's requirements of me. It's like I have minimum awareness of my needs. On a good day, I feel strong, fearless, empowered, balanced and centred. Oh, and I'm learning to know that I'm beautiful inside and out, but I think this is going to take some practice.

Session 12

I seem to have a permanent headache. I flit between pretending I'm okay and being busy (default position) to being furious or really wanting to cry. I don't seem to know how to get rid of this feeling. There's a pressure cooker where my brain used to be.

I keep thinking about the concept of forgiveness. I don't know what I think, I don't know if I can, if I want to, or if I need to. I've read (almost) everywhere that this is required for total healing to take place. My therapist said it was one way to look at it but maybe there were others. She believed healing could happen in many ways, to not worry about that for now. I found this so reassuring.

Session 25

I hit a sticky wicket in therapy today. I think my therapist started to feel she didn't know what to do with me. She was identifying how much I was trying to process everything in my head. She said something like, 'I sometimes feel stuck with you. It's like every attempt I make to get into those deeper parts of you, you bat me away like tennis. You seem so stuck in your head most of the time, comparing yourself to others relentlessly against ridiculously high standards you set yourself, I just don't know what to do with you sometimes to get in.'

She was sharing her experience to help the process (a common therapeutic tool). I talked about my frustration with things not moving faster in therapy and about not feeling able to let go of 'it', whatever it is, although feeling desperately like I wanted to. What is this damn 'IT'? Was I still holding up my guard, even here, even now?

She asked if I wanted to go to court and I said I was petrified. She asked what about, and I couldn't think how to explain. Shame, worry I won't be believed or made out to be deserving of it happening to me, that it was my fault. I was still trying to be strong to the outside world to hold it all together, afraid of my breakdown.

We had a breakthrough moment though. She said to me, 'Know that you are doing exactly what you need to do to help you move forward and it's exactly enough for you right now.' The weight lifted immediately. It was like a magic sentence. 'You are exactly where you're meant to be right now, and it's okay.' One tiny sentence, just like that. I had been looking for the ta-dah moment, and also holding the entire load of responsibility with me. I noticed the next day I even stopped giving myself a hard time. It was wonderful. Such freedom.

Session 28
What a difference a week can make.

Back for therapy and I genuinely feel like I'm getting back to my old self again. Only a better version. My therapist even observed I looked better/different. She said it was the first time I'd actually sat back on the sofa relaxed and that I looked softer somehow. She used the word 'wholesome' to describe me. I wasn't sure what I felt about that word, it seemed to imply ruddy-cheeked and made me think of *Darling Buds of May*, a round robust farmer's wife (or perhaps she meant Catherine Zeta Jones?) But there's my self-analysis about not being good enough and comparing popping up again. I jumped straight to 'Great! I'm fixed (ta-dah), time to give it a rest now, then.'

And we both laughed. I'm so desperate to feel fixed, to be at the end of the painful part. It's really hard sitting with the parts of you that you don't like.

The rest of the session we talked about relationships, how I often showed up as their girl-friend, sister-like role, not an item of infatuation or love. This was clearly my choice. I'm hoping the next few sessions help me to continue reconnecting with my female foxy, sassy, loving, beautiful, vulnerable version of me. Where the hell has she been hiding all these years?

I'm also noticing a different relationship with my body. I like it more. In fact, I've noticed I've even been checking myself out in the mirror (something I would never do).

Session 32

Two days from my thirty-seventh birthday and I'm totally unexcited. It used to be I loved my birthday, but these days they serve to remind me I'm not where I want to be in life. That I'm single. I can't help feeling bitterly jealous of everyone settled with a family of their own or just in relationships. Grass is always greener, I guess. I feel like life is going backwards for me some days. Sometimes there's so much in my head I feel I could still be writing in seven days' time having not had a rest and still only be touching the surface.

Downton Abbey is tackling rape this series. It's touching, moving, disturbing and upsetting for me to see. They've picked up on the whole issue of shame quite well, I think. I observe the victim being supported by her husband and told that she's loved and she's not damaged goods. I feel sad I didn't have that or didn't believe it until now. Maybe I still need some work. I'm struggling again with my sense of self-love and the relationship I have with my body.

Session 48

Went back to see my therapist today after my acupuncture practitioner helped me realise I was getting in the way of the process, keeping us at a head level, not allowing us to go deeper into the body. I asked my therapist to help me connect with my body and the wisdom in it, to connect with the trauma stored there.

It was fascinating. I felt a pain in my sternum first, like I was crushed, suffocating. I couldn't breathe, then noticed that my legs were tense but senseless, like they were numb. My whole body below the waist felt paralysed. I realised my vagina felt scared (I know, this seems weird to me too), but there was an awareness of fear there. My body was on high alert, unloved, alone and uncared for. Golly, this was also my doing. I had been ignoring it, not listening to what it wanted from me, the nourishing, nurturing kind of love.

I cried a lot in this session. It felt nice. I think a genuine release happened. I've learnt that feeling fixed is not a destination we arrive at, we are all broken in some way. No one gets through life without experiencing some collateral damage. On some level our needs for survival, love and connection will not be met all of the time and this affects our core, our soul, our sense of self. I have been fortunate that I found a fantastic therapist and had a wonderful acupuncture practitioner who guided me to therapy in the first place (despite my objections). In looking at our core wounds we can take a journey to healing, but this doesn't equate to feeling fixed. It's a greater sense of self, of who we really are, or who we were always meant to be before we wrapped ourselves up in so much body armour we started to shut out the world.

I learnt it's important not to judge anything in the process of self-exploration, just know it is what it is and there is no right or wrong, only what you feel and think in those moments. Therapy became a safe haven for me to explore my darkest thoughts, to reconnect with my treasured dreams, to learn to be me.

8. The Breakdown

'Waking up to who you are requires letting go of who you imagine yourself to be.'
ALAN WATTS

Trauma, or the memory of it, can keep its own check of time, and however hard you try to forget about it or lock it away, another part of you knows it still exists in your being somewhere. It's not uncommon for victims of abuse to experience a 'seasonal' breakdown, particularly around the anniversary of the trauma itself.

For me, summer was always an emotional rollercoaster ride, but this year would feel different because now the lid was off Pandora's box and I was getting stuck in. Everything was somehow more raw. What would follow my breakdown was, in fact, two breakthroughs, and this stands testament to the belief that when you really commit to therapy and go to the places you're most afraid of, you can find your biggest treasure.

There came a time about eighteen months into my weekly therapy sessions where I really hit rock bottom. I was surprising myself that I was still committed to going to therapy having spent years looking for that elusive quick fix. It was the anniversary of the rape and I was five weeks away from appearing in court. The summer turmoil usually appeared in a regular pattern for me. At some point in June, I consciously think, 'Hang on, its nearly time for the anniversary, brace yourself'. Then somehow I go into my usual busy life, throwing myself into anything and everything and I temporarily forget.

At some point into July, the tears start (more than normal), unexplained frustration and anger at everything and anyone (but mainly myself), which is of course unvented (except at myself). The sabotage of self usually includes a slowing down of exercise or a doubling up on efforts; healthy eating falls away, drinking increases and a feeling of doom descends on me. Nothing and no one seem to make it better. Of course from the outside you wouldn't notice, such was my skill for putting on a brave face. I'm perhaps a little quieter, more secluded than usual, but otherwise to the outside eye I'm no different. The pain is internal, just like the attack.

Somewhere throughout the summer I get used to it and I get used to pretending it's okay, until the heat of summer falls away into autumn, the nights get cooler and the self-sabotage recedes. I can't tell you how much I bloody love autumn. Somehow I'm able to let go. Until next year anyway.

This particular year I was hoping it would be my last. I saw the court case as symbolic of letting go, Finally I was doing something, and hopefully it would be my last angry sabotage. I felt determined that I would no longer allow this pattern to re-enter my life. I'd do whatever it took.

I had also committed to long-term therapy. Through this, I'd been doing a lot of work on myself, I had an improved level of self-belief and self-love and I was taking better care of myself and my wellbeing than I ever had before. Of course this year would be different, I was finally facing my past, putting right the wrongs that had been done. I was also recovering from a heartbreak. I had just lost what I thought was the love of my life. I had finally shown up different in this relationship, most likely as a result of the therapy. I seemed more able to express and communicate myself, to show up vulnerable and for that to feel okay, to speak my truth, to offer my love wholeheartedly and unconditionally. Sadly, it hadn't been enough. Sprinkle on top of that the impending court case, the tension and fear which builds, and you have a triple whammy.

Rock bottom happened.

I shared with my therapist that I'd felt hopeless enough a lot of the time to think about ending my life. I don't think I had any intention of doing it, it was more a reflection of the level of hopelessness I had reached. It's not that I wanted to die, I really didn't, there was lots I still wanted to achieve. I just didn't know how to do all that with these feelings of loss surrounding me. I had arrived at the bottom of the deep black pit in my heart I had been avoiding all these years, determined to survive without having to open Pandora's box. Now I was there, I had no idea if I'd ever get out. I felt trapped by myself, isolated and broken. I had endured enough pain and I was ready to take the only option I felt I had to run away from it. I was tired of fighting it. However much effort and work I put into fixing me, it didn't make it go away, the shame, the hurt, the pain, feeling damaged.

In that deep and dark place, I acquired a level of empathy for those people who make the decision to end their lives. The hopelessness can feel suffocating. You feel like a burden on your family and friends. Fortunately for me, I chose life. By my nature I'm a fixer, a sorter of problems, an optimist (which probably meant sitting with this darkness all the more tough). For me it's like asking a dancer not to dance. It's the opposite of my psyche. To get to the point where even Mrs Resourceful can't find one thing to do to help fix it was like hell for me.

There was something quite grounding about sharing this information with my therapist, although I felt ashamed at the time, to consider the waste of such a precious life, a precious opportunity. But that was how I felt in that moment and I'd perhaps not even been aware that it had got that bad, such was my denial. That was my truth right there in that room. And it seemed like it was a surprise to my therapist.

I think, as victims, we learn to live with the hopelessness and know that like the rollercoaster ride, there will be higher times and lower times. What would follow the breakdown was another breakthrough; in fact, two. The first was the realisation that at a deep level I didn't feel recognised for who I was or able to express that side of me with real meaning and authenticity. The second was an incredible ability to not accept warmth, comfort or empathy from others. I was unable to take it in; I mean really take it in. I had as such locked myself away from harm so much that on some deeper level of my unconscious I'd actually surrounded myself with a forcefield big enough to deter the Millennium Falcon.

As I sat in the therapist's cosy room, my hand held in hers as I sobbed, she squeezed my hand, wanting me to know she was there for me, that she finally understood my pain at a deep and real level and wanted to help me heal. All I could feel was the physical touch of her squeeze on my hand. She asked me if I could feel her hand and noted that I was not holding her hand in return. She asked where I felt the warmth of her touch and I noted I had no feeling beyond my wrist. It was the most surreal experience, and it saddened me. To meet me, I'm a really warm friendly, talk-to-anyone kind of girl. This comes naturally to me; I was always a giver of warmth. So to discover that not only have I not been expressing myself wholeheartedly, but I also wasn't able to receive her empathy in this moment froze my heart over. It would be the breakthrough I needed to enable me to learn to receive and ask for help and support. To let people in, to really let them in at a deep level.

It really was that moment I'd read about, a key turning point in therapy, the rock bottom point, facing 'it' in all its ugliness, connecting with it, loving it, accepting it and allowing it to release whatever emotion it held. Then you're able to let go. To feel differently. That's where the shift occurs.

Some people survive quite happily in life never having any therapy; they're able to shut the box and find joy where they can. But for me, there's something about my mind that needs to understand, to make sense and to be able to turn it into something positive. I'm not willing to just accept things as they are. I'm not willing to waste this precious life of mine either. We're here on this planet in this body for actually a very short time and I want to make mine count. I wanted to thrive, not just survive.

9. Waiting

'In any given moment we have two options: to step forward into growth or to step back in safety.'
ABRAHAM MASLOW

The investigation of my case by the police took over one year, and I can tell you that patience is not one of my biggest strengths. Historical cases are always deprioritised in favour of current cases or cases affecting a minor, which is how it should be. Sadly, for me, that meant it was a waiting game. I tried to get on with life, throwing myself into everything I could with gusto, but it was like someone else was in control of the pause button, and it appeared to be stuck down. I remember feeling like I was wearing those child safety reins, desperately wanting to push on forward, but a grey cloud was following me around everywhere on the other end of them.

Then eventually the police called … 'We want to put forward your rape case to CPS as we think there's enough evidence to get a conviction in court. Are you happy to proceed?' *Holy Hell!* A timid 'Yes' (I think) came out.

I had never set out to go to court. I thought the furthest it would go would be the police and a polite conversation with the attacker. Now it really did feel out of my hands. The police also told me they'd investigated the case of abuse from when I was younger and had concluded there wasn't enough evidence to prosecute the babysitter, but they did believe me that it happened.

Being told that people believe you has been one of the most important aspects to this experience of healing for me – being acknowledged. Sometimes it's hard to take it in and I feel like I want to brush it off, but when I've given myself permission to take it in, boy, does it feel good. Emotional, yes, but healing mostly.

It was bitter sweet to hear that one was being proceeded with but the other wasn't. It was tough hearing that the case of the babysitter would go no further, that the individual was already in prison (for other non-related crimes). I felt sad. I felt sad that he'd chosen that path, but I also had a sense that he was being punished already and felt able to let it go (for now anyway).

From that point onwards, it was no longer about me. I was merely a key witness in a case of the Crown. I didn't like this part of the process. It fed my hopelessness because I wasn't in control. I got through it because I remained focused on the bigger picture: I'm doing the right thing. I was trying to make the world a safer place. For me, I was ready to have my day in court and say publicly, 'WHAT YOU DID TO ME WAS WRONG. I NO LONGER ACCEPT IT.'

Waiting for the court day was like a super level upgrade in my patience training programme. We were allocated a date in July 2014 which was a six-month wait. Then, a month before, it got pushed back a month to August 2014. Four days before the case was about to start in August, it was postponed again, this time for six months back to

February 2015.

The second cancellation hit hard. I had been delivering work in London all day and was getting on the train at Kings Cross to return home. I received a call to my mobile; it was Witness Support. My heart fell off the platform to the tracks. I knew straight away.

'They're changing the date again, aren't they?'

'I'm so sorry, yes,' came the reply.

I was stunned, I genuinely couldn't believe it. I had been waiting just short of two years already and had spent the last two months feeling overwhelmed and consumed by the presence of this date we were all building up to. My life had felt on hold, unable to see beyond 'the date'. My usual flurry of planning and scheming adventures, making plans for exciting weekends away, time with friends all suspended for this period and beyond, focusing on surviving without falling apart.

The light at the end of the tunnel had been so near I could almost touch it and although I was dreading the actual day in court, I just wanted it to be over. The sweet tempting fact that I could almost taste, taste life, that I'd be able to start getting on with living again, that the priority would be me not this damn case. That I'd finally have my closure.

To be told just six days away from it happening that it was being postponed again, I hadn't been prepared. Everything had pointed to it happening and although I knew there was still a chance it could get postponed, my instinct told me it was going to happen. The truth is that a case can get postponed on the actual day of the trial if something else that warrants a greater risk to society comes along.

A new date had been pencilled in: six months away! Another blow to the heart. Six months? I didn't think I could take the pressure of waiting for that much longer.

The volcano in my heart (so well known to me by now) started to bubble and then erupt and the tears of lava started seeping out of my eyes, stinging them on their release. They were sad and angry tears. I tried to repress them, conscious that other passengers were boarding the train, but they kept coming out. The other suits on the train sitting near to me peered over from time to time. No one spoke to ask if I was okay, and I was grateful. Two tissues later I sat hot in my seat, the lava tears still seeping out one by one as slowly they hardened and my tears turned to anger, which turned to rage. I wanted to stick my head in my hands and collapse onto the table in front of my seat and sob, but there were three other passengers sitting at the table with me.

Twenty minutes later, a gin and tonic and a packet of salty crisps from the snack cabin brought me round and I had a moment of clarity: it felt like another part of me was talking, that voice again, the one you sometimes hear in your head and wonder if it's you or some weird divine intervention. I heard it say, 'No more. No more of this feeling sorry for yourself. It's not helpful. This stupid event cannot dominate your life. From now on, you and only you are the number one priority here. So what do you need?'

It was a kind voice and I still don't know where it came from, but I listened. It was another breakthrough moment for me. Immediately, I thought, *I need a break, I need to GIVE myself a break*, and I started being kinder to myself. It was what it was; there was nothing I could do to dispute it.

So I made a pact with myself. I was sick of feeling scared and I was sick of feeling sorry for myself. From now on, the first priority is me and my happiness, which means the least priority in my life is this damn case. From this moment forward (as best I'm able to), I get back in the driving seat and do what I've always done best. I get busy living and I tackle this with the same positivity I've tried to tackle all aspects of my life.

One of the biggest lessons I share with coaching and acupuncture clients is that we always have a choice. Your feelings don't choose you, you choose them. A feeling is often your body's way of responding to what you're thinking. So if you think shit thoughts, you'll get shit feelings. Imagine your brain is like Google: what you put in the search box, your brain will go looking for. Wake up and think, *I'm going to have a shit day today* and your brain-google will go looking for all the things that could make it shit. Try putting in *I'm going to have a great day* and your Google will look for all the evidence to show you it's great.

I know from my own experience that the dark days are tough and you're entitled to have those days, roll around in the mud, feel sad, cry it out, but just don't stay there too long or unsupported. We don't always feel like we're in control a lot of the time, but we are in control of us and how we choose to feel. No one can make us feel anything we don't choose ourselves.

In the next phase of waiting, I really got to know my IDAS support worker. IDAS are a charity organisation originally set up to support victims of domestic abuse. Their services in North Yorkshire have now expanded to support victims of sexual abuse regardless of the situation. People can contact IDAS independently of any court or police process; their main priority is the victims, however long ago their trauma was.

My contact at IDAS was fantastic. She understood the court process, the police process, what would happen on the day. She told me about other people and what they'd found had helped them and she got me thinking about afterwards too, which I hadn't even considered at this point. She could answer any question I had and was there when I needed her, but she let me feel in control of how often and when we met. She was happy to come to my house, and even put up with my new puppy weeing on her trouser leg on one occasion (oh, the shame!).

10. The Themes of Abuse

'Write hard and clear about what hurts.'
Ernest Hemingway

I struggled for a long time to make sense of what had happened to me, what I had decided to do about it and how it was affecting me now. My feelings were dark and all consuming, feelings of being alone, feeling trapped, helpless, hopeless, ruined, insignificant, the turmoil, the battles. I tried to make sense of my experience in the lonely isolated world I had created (unknowingly) through journalling and writing poetry.

I remember finding the concept of what if all of life's events were happening FOR you, not TO you? What if even the bad stuff was happening to help you grow? And wondering how you could ever turn abuse into a gift, for what purpose could it ever serve beyond trauma and pain?

It didn't sit well with me. When I first came across it on a personal development course, I remember feeling so enraged at the thought of it being a gift I'd had to leave the auditorium (mid-conference) to get air. I felt grief welling up in me like a tidal wave, one I had no control of. I ended up falling to my knees in angry tears on a nearby golf course. Thankfully, I found one of the coaches and we talked it through. She helped me to see that perhaps my younger abuser, as a seventeen-year-old himself, had been surrounded by less privileged beliefs and less love whilst growing up. That perhaps something similar may have happened to him, that his role models were not great ones. I remember feeling a swell of compassion for him that I didn't understand at the time. I wanted to wrap up the little boy version of him and tell him it would be okay, that there was another way, that I was sorry he hadn't been born into a stronger, wiser family, that he hadn't been taught how to respect humans, including himself.

I would later realise that being raped had indeed given me many gifts. It had helped me to become a coach, to do the work I do now making a difference to people's lives as I'd spent years trying to understand people by studying every book, course, approach I could to help myself heal. It contributed to my sensory acuity which was so much more switched on, which meant I could connect with people more quickly. It made me stronger, braver than I ever imagined I might be. It turned up my intuition and gave me the belief of trust.

On the other hand, two of my Achilles heels are helplessness and hopelessness. When I feel down or stuck or unable to find the answer I start to feel helpless and hopeless, which takes me straight to victim territory. It's hard for me to be there.

Since I started to speak out more about my experience it's been amazing how many people have spoken out to me about their own experience; heart warming and humbling and also sad at the same time. It would seem there were common threads between us, similar themes in how our experiences have shaped how we live and turn up in the world. Just sharing how those events had impacted us made us realise we were not alone. We were not weird; we were actually very normal.

I had experienced the benefit of therapy and so had gone some way to understanding I was normal and that these 'patterns' were consistent with victims of abuse, and now I was able to offer that to others who might need the reassurance. It has helped keep me motivated to write this book, like the universe was showing me that people (like me) needed this book, needed hope too.

Sabotage was a big theme for me, particularly through my twenties, particularly with regards to relationships. I would find someone lovely and usually I would ruin the relationship or not even allow myself to be in it. The minute it started to feel too intimate and loving, I would end it.

On some level, for me I didn't think I deserved to be happy in a relationship. I believed deep down I was damaged goods and I was petrified I would be found out and be abandoned, so I would usually abandon them first. I wasn't loving all of me, so how could they? Of course, consciously I wasn't aware that this pattern was playing out but I was aware I had a sadness about what I was pushing away. It's so ironic that that which we crave the most we keep furthest away from us. Slowly taking steps to learn to love all of me would be a game changer in my process of recovery.

Abandonment was another theme I discovered through therapy. Having been left on both occasions in the care of someone else, I had learnt from an early age that no one else could guarantee my safety. They wouldn't always be there to take care of me. I should learn to take care of myself and only rely on myself. On some level I was creating a reality of abandonment to confirm the story my subconscious had learnt: that I would always be alone.

The flipside to abandonment is fierce independence. I found it incredibly hard to let people help me. I was almost incapable of asking for help. I'd surrounded myself with a bubble of self-protection and so no one had a chance of getting in. I used to joke that mine was double armoured, bullet proof, SAS protected. Imagine anyone trying to offer me help and being able to receive it with that belief and level of body armour? Yep, no one stood a chance of making it through the first wall. And so I became ridiculously resourceful and independent, usually playing the helper, giver, caring role so I didn't have to receive.

Again, therapy really helped me to identify where and how this was showing up for me, and once you're aware enough of the pattern you can take control of your response to it. It takes practice, but it is possible.

'Loving ourselves' was perhaps one of the hardest themes for me to get my head around and it's something that still takes daily practice. The self-abuse about not being good enough was as normal as getting up in the morning and brushing my teeth. Nothing was ever good enough. I was never the right shape, haircut, colour, height, weight, looks, intelligence, funny, the list went on and on and on.

I didn't like myself because I didn't want to. I was frightened of being attractive – what if it attracted more unwanted attention? I would overeat when I was stressed and put on weight. I would then kill myself in the gym, abusing my body in another way to counteract the first abuse. These days I have learnt to love what and who I am. I take time every day to look in the mirror and tell myself, 'You are more than enough'. I spend time every day on self-care, even if it's just taking an extra ten minutes to put body lotion on and I write my gratitude lists whenever I'm feeling a little insecure. It's work in progress of course and probably will be for some time yet, and that's okay.

Restlessness I believe is as a result of fear. Having been attacked, there is always a background awareness that the threat of danger could be just around the corner. For me, the times when you're at peace or sleeping had been ruined as they were no longer safe places, having been attacked twice in bed. My sensory acuity is so switched on as a result of what happened to me, I can hear a leaf drop. In fact, sometimes it's so switched on I actually find it hard to turn off. So put me in a busy room and I hear everything, which makes focusing on the conversation in front of me really tough sometimes.

I also have a remarkable ability to notice the slightest change in someone's facial expression and to pick up on emotional shifts. I'm observant beyond belief. This is the flight or fight survival part of my brain which has been turned up to full throttle to make sure that no further attacks are received.

All these skills I now see as both a gift (they help me to show up as an intuitive coach), but also a curse (sleeping at night can be a problem). Learning to turn them up or down as I need them has been really helpful. Havening would turn out to be a killer tool in helping me address my fearful panic attacks. (Oddly, I was so used to them I hadn't even labelled them as panic attacks.)

Havening is a therapeutic tool used by coaches and therapists that works on your brain's neural pathways. The process creates new neurons to replace old ones which have been programmed unhelpfully. For me, it literally reprogrammed my flight/fight receptors to respond to normal levels, so I was no longer behaving like a soldier when the wind tapped the window. I could be aware of my safety without the physiological response of anxiety and panic kicking in as an auto responder from my body.

Shame would turn out to be a shadow theme from my abuse, one I didn't want to acknowledge. It was Brené Brown's book *Daring Greatly* about vulnerability that helped me connect, unpick and grow from this awareness. Brené Brown is a social researcher who has published many books and she specialises in researching the topics of vulnerability, shame and courage. The only people who create shame are ourselves. It's ironic because we believe that other people will judge us if only they knew our dirty secrets or that we're not good enough, not perfect. So in doing so, we're actually judging ourselves and choosing a place of shame.

In the book, *Daring Greatly*, Brené Brown oulines three steps to shame resilience: practice courage and reach out; talk to yourself the way you would someone you really loved; own the story – don't let it fester or define you. Brené Brown's work would be life changing for me as it helped me take the steps I needed in therapy and to be braver than I thought possible when approaching the police. Her work taught me to embrace my vulnerability, that it was perhaps one of my most precious gifts.

Fundamentally I needed to be able to return the blame that belonged with my attacker to him and keep the part that I was responsible for. This would eventually happen, but long after the court case was concluded.

I had disowned a part of me (I'm still not sure which part, perhaps it was many), on a physical level most definitely my genital area, on an emotional level perhaps my femininity. I was fearful that my 'femaleness' had attracted this unwanted attention in the first place, so to deny it may keep me safe. Also the part of me that hadn't shouted (that was in shock). I wasn't very proud of that part of me; it had let me down and that part chose shame. So on some deep level, I disowned parts of me which meant I didn't love all of me. Learning to love myself (all of myself) would be a crucial part in my healing journey.

It took me a long time, with my therapist's support, to re-engage my ability to receive help, to provide self-love and also to be able to ask for help (and not feel guilty). People want to help, and eventually I realised it was selfish of me to be a helper and not let other people help me if they wanted. My life has definitely become richer as a result of this growth.

I had always been aware of a fear of being too girly, but I had never really understood it fully. To the outside eye, I dressed like a woman, had curves, wasn't ashamed of my body, was even foxy some of the time, but I knew deep down I wasn't embracing the softer more feminine, girly side of me. I was frightened of her.

I had worked for fifteen years in a very male-dominated industry and to get ahead I embraced even more of my masculine energy; the driven, focused, make shit happen side of me. I also knew I had built my virtual wall around me. It was there to protect me, so softening into my girl would require me to lower the wall. Something I wasn't sure about at all. It reignited all my fears about attracting the wrong kind of attention.

Flamenco was my first foray into this new discovery of my true feminine self. I had decided to attend dance classes, wanting to connect more with the activities I'd loved growing up. Singing and dancing were massive parts of my life, and having spent many childhood holidays in Spain watching traditional flamenco, I decided this would be my new dance. Something about the female dancers when they were in their strong poses appealed to me; they were strong but they were also feminine. They had both, and as a dance flamenco embodies the perfect balance of masculine and feminine energy, the balance of submission and dominance, of giving and receiving. It teaches you to play with this spectrum, to find your own place. It would be the start of me softening into my true self.

It wasn't until my second Tony Robbins experience, *Date with Destiny*, just before the court case eventually happened, that I would truly begin to discover my feminine energy and just what I had been holding back. Tony Robbins is an American life coach who runs personal development experiences over several days. They're intense, long days grounded in the belief that anything is possible with the right personal state and mindset. For so many people, these events are life changing.

Day three of the *Date with Destiny* event was relationship day. I would learn that although as humans we all prioritise two of the same six human needs (certainty, variety, love, significance, contribution and growth), on a day-to-day basis, women and men also have different primary drivers. For men, freedom was important. Although they want to be loved, they need to have their freedom too, and scenes from *Braveheart* were blasted throughout the auditorium to bring that masculine energy of freedom to life, with Mel Gibson shouting '*They may take our lives, but they will never take our FREEDOM*'.

When it was time to discuss women Tony asked the men in the room to raise their hand if they'd been aware of their safety in the last twelve months. Maybe 5% of the men in the room lifted their hand (there were 10,000 people at this event, probably 50/50 men to women split). He asked the same question to the women and almost 100% of the women in the room lifted their hand. This was closely followed by a loud male gasp. Tony asked the women to keep their hands lifted if this was also true since they'd been at this event, and at least 40% of the women in the room still had their hand in the air. The men practically fell apart as they realised that we women in the room had felt unsafe in their presence.

Tony went on to explain that safety is women's primary need, that all the time women are aware that they're the prey and men are the predators. He went on to say that women therefore need to hear and feel reassured 'all the f***king time'. I knew fear was a big underlying driver for me, but I didn't want to accept it. To accept it meant I needed to connect with it and let go of feeling strong, being brave, staying safe. I was frightened. I realised the braver thing to do was to connect back to my feminine.

I went on to read lots more about feminine and masculine energy after this event and made a promise to myself to connect more with my feminine energy every day. I try to wear softer fabrics, to be softer in my body, to ask for and receive help, to be willing to share more of me. In fact, when I first returned I spent the first month laughing at myself saying 'soften, soften, swish, swish' in my head as I was walking around town, trying to focus on releasing the stiffness and tension that often sat across my chest. I noticed people looking at me differently, like they were seeing me for the first time rather than the invisible me I'd been hiding behind. Or perhaps I was just meeting a part of myself for the first time in a long while.

There are of course other themes (control, justice and fairness, self-harm). We're all different so our 'patterns' or 'themes' will vary for each of us. These are just some of the key ones I have experienced. It may be different for all of us in some way because it's not just the events themselves but also our upbringing, our parents and the support models we had available to us while growing up, and other influences in our lives like our friends, teachers, guides that influence who we become and how we show up.

11. All the thank yous

'Your naked body should only belong to those who fall in love with your naked soul.'

Charlie Chaplin

When I was very young all I wanted to be when I grew up was a mummy and a wife. My favourite game involved taking care of all my teddies and dolls. My going to bed routine at the age of seven always required a slightly longer period of time to make sure all the dolls and teddies (some fifteen plus) were tucked up in bed, warm, cosy and comfy. As I got older my ambitions started to grow: a teacher, the next female prime minister, a pilot, a lawyer. My dad repeatedly told me 'The world's your oyster, you can be whatever you choose to be'. Yet underneath it all, I knew my heart yearned to be a mummy and a wife mostly. I almost assumed it would just happen, it was nature after all. It seemed like the most natural thing in the world.

As I write this book, I'm thirty eight and single. I've had relationships, flings, one night stands. My longest relationship was two years. I've never been married, never been proposed to and never lived with my significant other. I am neither proud or ashamed of these facts, they are what they are and they could be the same regardless of my life experiences. Relationships just never seemed to work out smoothly for me. I think I knew deep down that the events of my past were of course having a massive impact on this part of my life and in some way I was sabotaging my own success. I just didn't want to accept it.

Dating today is different. More people choose to be single, to maintain their independence. But for me, being in a relationship was all I desperately wanted. I was successful beyond my expectations in everything else I put my mind to in life, but I just couldn't seem to meet the right one or be able to make it last. I've been connected to some lovely men in my life and I really believe a big part of it not working out with any of them was because on some deeper level, I just didn't love myself enough. Timing probably played a key part with some. But a part of me felt broken and if I didn't love me then how could someone else?

People used to say to me 'You just need to learn to love yourself' and I felt the desire to punch them in the face. I really didn't get it. Of course I love myself, I thought, in my mind irritated by their commentary on my life. I was successful, attractive, had great friends and family, funny, smart, loving. Heck, I was even passionate (despite my traumatic experiences). But they were right, another part of me much deeper didn't love all of me. It didn't love the broken parts. And so I tried to conquer the world by proving to myself that I could do more, be more, have more. Fundamentally I didn't believe I was enough.

I have had relationships, I have fallen in love, I've experienced sexual intimacy with another I never dreamt possible. I've also got my fair share of bad date stories and relationships that never should have gone on as long as they did.

For a long time I believed it was the trauma I had experienced that got in the way of the relationship I desired. Then I started my journey with therapy and I realised it was so much more complex than that. Life is a rich tapestry which has many loose threads. Did the events of abuse and rape affect my ability to connect and love myself? Yes, most definitely. Did those events affect my ability to trust, open my heart, feel safe with another man in an intimate relationship? Of course they did. And what I also now know to be true is that it's not *just* those events which affect our ability to give and receive love. Our very early childhood, the nature of our birth into the world, whether we were loved appropriately by our parents or those closest to us as we developed into human beings, the relationships we did and didn't have, our experience of friendships which worked and those that didn't, all these things (and much more) affect how we're able to offer and receive love.

Being able to see that my relationship status was more complex than I first thought allowed me to take some pressure off the cause and effect line I had drawn between my single status to the trauma. When I looked back over all the heartbreaks I had experienced with my therapist's gentle support I saw for the first time that they each in some way had contributed to helping piece back together my broken parts and I felt a wave of gratitude for every tear I'd ever cried over them.

- My first boyfriend (after the rape) taught me that I was desirable, and he would also be my first 'proper' consensual sexual experience. He took care of me, treated me with respect and showed me what consensual sex should be like.
- My boyfriend at university showed me that although I felt bro-

ken in some way, I was also normal and loveable. He was wonderful, kind, funny, caring, smart, genuine. I kept him at arm's length, ashamed of my secret. He taught me I needed to be able and willing to share what had happened to me if I wanted to let love in.

- The first boyfriend after university taught me to stop comparing myself to others and judging myself as unworthy. He saw and showed me I had a foxy side. He started to show me that I too was attractive, both inside and out and that I shouldn't be afraid of how I looked.

- A few one night stands followed. Not many, but more than I'd like to recount. I wasn't respecting my body, so why should they? I had learned to keep men at arm's length. It was safer that way. They would never find out how damaged I was and decide to not like me. These events taught me (painfully) that another person would not respect me and my boundaries if I wasn't respecting them myself. Thank you to you all!

- My first work boyfriend I pushed away. I was starting to feel some greater self worth and I knew he adored me. Whilst it felt nice I couldn't take it in, I felt like a fraud. By rejecting his love for me he taught me I was rejecting and hurting him too. That was a tough lesson to learn.

- Then a long while later a wonderful boyfriend helped me to enjoy my body with boundaries, taught me how important it was to communicate what I did and didn't want when having sex. He was bold, brave, sensitive, kind and utterly respectful of me and my body. He taught me a love that didn't need words. I previously hadn't been very good at speaking up when it came to sex, trying to go with the flow rather than 'own' my part in it, still trying to work out what was appropriate or inappropriate and where my needs sat within this dance. This boyfriend really opened the doors for me to start loving all of me again and he taught me so much more than he'll ever know. Ironically, the biggest lesson he taught me was that by focussing on trying to love him more than loving myself I would surely suffocate any relationship that existed between us. He taught me I needed to love myself and trust that the relationship will be what it's meant to be.

Although I am currently single (at the time of writing), I have more hope in my heart about what is possible for me in a loving relationship than I ever have before based on the following beliefs I hold as a result of my journey and the people who have contributed to it:

- I know that we should make choices based on what we believe and know is right for us, not what someone else says or does; that we should tune into our intuition and learn to communicate from that place.
- That we are free and empowered to decide what we do and don't want, how important it is to know and uphold our boundaries.
- That soulmates do exist (I have found two already and there is still time to discover more).
- That you can re-learn what it means to have a healthy respectful and enjoyable sex life with someone you love after you've been raped.
- That we're capable of learning to trust again.
- That learning to love yourself is definitely the key (despite my

earlier protestations, those damn wise people were flipping right).

- Healthy boundaries, unconditional love and open communication from the heart is the key to a successful relationship.

Trauma does not need to wreck your entire life. With the right support, the right mindset and a little time and kindness, you can have what you always dreamt of. And I know my role as a sassy wife and a loving mother in my own unique way will happen one day somehow. There is always hope. From every relationship that didn't work out, I learnt something about me, about being in a relationship, about connecting to even more love.

12. Preparing for D-day

'You are braver than you believe, stronger than you seem, smarter than you think, and loved more than you'll ever know.'

A.A. Milne

Getting ready for appearing in court was stressful enough in itself. It wasn't a local court, so we'd have to travel. None of us had ever appeared in a court before and we had no idea what to expect. We were advised that we could do a pre-court visit, so back when we thought the case was going to happen in August, my parents and I decided to book a day and take advantage of this preparation (or rather I decided it would be a good idea for me and invited my parents to support me). I wanted no surprises on the day and no more trauma than I was already expecting to endure.

As a key witness in a case about rape, I was entitled to special measures in court, such as a screen so I wouldn't need to see my attacker, the accused. There is also a special entrance and private room for victims so I didn't have to worry about bumping into my attacker when I arrived at court. We didn't want any surprises on the day; I wanted to be reassured as best I could.

The pre-visit helped me greatly to prepare for the main event. My parents and I drove over for the lunch break, our allocated time to visit. Our objective was simple: know how to get there, know where to go when we arrive, get a sense of the room to prepare ourselves mentally, then leave. Bish bash bosh.

We were shown the private witness waiting rooms for those victims where they wouldn't want to bump into the accused. It was small, windowless, lacking in atmosphere, but at least it was safe and we'd all be together for the waiting part anyway.

We made our way up to a courtroom so I could see what the room would be like, to visualise myself there and prepare. I was calm but irritated. Irritated that I was having to give up a day for this visit. Irritated that I should even have been put in this position in the first place. But although it seemed like a practical visit, it turned out to be quite emotional.

As we waited in the octagonal waiting area outside of the courtrooms with the local criminals, most of whom were awaiting their sentence, I started to feel nauseous. My legs had taken on a jelly-like quality. This didn't feel like a place I belonged. My eyes started to feel hot, prickly tears were coming. All the while, the man giving us the tour was talking away going through all the advice and information my IDAS lady had already talked me through. All I heard was blah blah blah blah.

Eventually we entered a courtroom. You don't know until the day which court your case will be in, so you have a look in any that are free. It was light, airy and spacious, not at all what I'd expected. I'd requested a screen so that I couldn't see the accused. I thought it would make it easier on the day if I didn't have to see him, to feel threatened or eyeballed in any way. I'd imagined the screen would be around him and the rest of the room open to me, but the screen was actually around me. On the day, I would only be able to see the judge and the jury. It felt odd.

It wasn't until the court case that we started to tell some more of the family: my closest two auntys and my Mum's brother, who didn't seem shocked. He knew my rapist as a part-time doorman on the pubs in Barnsley and didn't have too high an opinion of him. We also told one of Dad's cousins who lived locally to us in York. We didn't want them reading it in the paper or finding out by other means. Although it was more 'out there', it also remained a taboo topic. Unless I brought it up, other people didn't mention it.

As the man in the court kept on explaining about the day, the order, the processes, what to expect, what to know about answering the questions, the witness box was drawing me in and the enormity of the situation engulfed me unexpectedly. The tears came, my heart started to pound so loud I couldn't hear anything else, my legs felt like jelly, disappearing from underneath me. I found the courage to call time out and turned on my heel heading for the door, looking for the escape route. There wasn't one. I was frozen. I felt trapped.

The sobs came, I couldn't breathe, I was having a panic attack. I didn't think I could do it. I remember saying over and over 'I can't do this, let me out, I can't do this'. I didn't know who this person was reacting like this, I was usually so contained, brave, fearless even, yet here I was breaking down. It was like the seventeen-year-old version of me had turned up and wanted nothing to do with it all.

Thankfully it passed after a few minutes and some careful breathing whilst trying to ignore the dotty volunteer that was repeatedly telling me how calm I will feel on the day. My poor mum had also started crying on seeing me upset and was being comforted by my dad. We were shown out by the back entrance that we'd use on the day when we arrived so that we had privacy and could avoid using the main door.

I had no idea I would feel like I did or react in the way I did, so I'm very glad I went along to the pre-visit. So were my parents. It also gave me a chance to have a little cry in advance. If it happens on the day then I'll be okay, I thought, because it's already happened once and I now know what to expect.

When we returned home, my dad realised that it had been 20 years to the date that the rape took place, which was a spooky coincidence we all thought. That breakdown in court really started to clear some of the pain for me and from that point onwards I gave myself even more permission to cry. And boy, did I cry; usually on my own, sometimes in therapy, sometimes I thought it would never end. It was healing me although I didn't understand that at the time.

I made a commitment to myself to make sure I meditated. This was something I had only just learnt to do, but felt it really helped me stay more calm and peaceful. On this particular day, as I was meditating, I had this awareness that my mind was erasing the emotion of the day as if on backward fast forward, scrambling the intensity of it. When I came out of my meditation, I felt totally different, like I'd been cleansed somehow. It was a very weird but welcome experience.

My survival kit for preparing for court:
I've learnt over the years there are some essential things I need for those days when it gets tough, and court days are super tough. I'm sure you'll have your own survival kit. It's worth just being more mindful

and notice what you head for when a wobble starts. It might be a fizzy sugary drink, for example, or a cigarette or a headache tablet, which of course come with their own issues. For me, it was like I needed to grab something, to feel resourceful, to do something to take hold of it all and I've been there when a cigarette seemed like a good idea. I made a conscious effort to find things that helped support me in a healthy way without being too new age about it!

Here are my top ten:

1. Tissues

I used to be the Margaret Thatcher Iron Lady of tear control until I started having therapy, and now, if they're coming, they're pretty much coming whether I like it or not. So tissues are a must as I can't stand a snotty runny nose, it's really not a good look on me.

2. Frankincense

An absolute wonder aromatherapy oil. A few drops on a tissue inhaled and it just brings me back together, helping me to feel grounded. It really is that amazing. So whenever I'm having a wobble, I'll inhale some of this little beauty and all will seem calmer and more grounded.

3. Citricidal

When I get stressed out, it goes straight to my tummy and for me everything gets stuck: I get heart burn, my tummy bloats, IBS kicks off, I can't seem to process my food efficiently, and without going into details my bottom starts to misbehave. A few drops of this in some water and it clears the stagnation. The same is true of apple cider vinegar. It tastes really bitter and vile, but it's well worth it and means there's no need for nasty over-the-counter stuff that bungs you up or keeps you on the toilet for days.

4. Best friends on speed dial

Perhaps the most important for me. Having one or two friends you know you can call regardless of the wobble size, whether it's a hint in the wind that something doesn't feel right or a total tornado. These are the friends that will never judge you, will hold a space for you to be whatever you need to be at that moment. Sometimes for me, there are times when I just need to be alone, but I also know that I ALWAYS feel better for talking to these friends.

5. Outdoor space

I need outdoor space. I need to feel free and I need to feel the wind and the elements on my face and around my head. I used to be in love with someone who needed to be on a mountain bike when life was tough. Well, mine is just being outside, preferably with nature and space. I totally get that being on top of a mountain thing some people have, or just having my bare feet on wet grass. It's grounding and helps you keep perspective. It's partly what made me get Murphy, my dog.

6. Relaxing baths

For a long time, I used to only have showers and then I rediscovered baths again thanks to some lovely Neal's Yard bath remedy a friend bought me. Now it's a weekly treat to light the candles, use lovely bubble bath, sometimes I even take a glass of wine and I just give myself full permission to relax. It's another form of meditation (as far as my definition of meditation goes) and a great way of demonstrating self-love.

7. Laughter or a night out

It's so true that some belly laughs can heal an awful lot of pain, and it's a good release for your soul; failing that, my favourite comedy series or film and snuggle down on the sofa to laugh my head off. It releases those happy hormones. I do actually believe you can fake a laugh and still create the feel-good factor.

8. Singing

One I keep for the car and the shower, but BOY do I feel better after having a good old croon to some belters. It's another release of emotion from my system. For me, singing releases my soul without me having to communicate what I'm feeling. I can't understand how that works either, but it does.

9. Yoga and meditation

So I have to admit although I've been doing yoga for a while, I'm a bit of a late comer to the meditation thing. Yoga really helps me connect with my body, to go inside, and the breathing is fantastic for helping you just be here in the day, the present. As for meditation, I'm a total convert. I found Effortless Meditation by Effortless Jo to be a fantastic and easy, accessible course and the lady that runs it has become a treasured friend.

10. Active meditation

For those days when it's just too hard to settle or be still and breathing can feel like a NASA training exercise, I turn to active meditation, either exercise or something like gardening, DIY, cooking, making stuff. My mind has to focus on the job in hand (which is never arduous, of course) and as a result it stops thinking about that which is making me feel overwhelmed. It's distraction of the pleasant kind.

I could go on ... but these are my essential top ten.

13. D-day

'Trust in your truth, it will be the best decision you ever make.'
MARTHA BECK

The actual day of the court case finally came around. After all the cancellations and changes I think none of us believed it would ever happen. Even on the day before I was expecting a phone call to say it was delayed again. There was much organising of who would travel with whom. It might seem trivial now but I remember it feeling like a really big deal at the time. We were all grappling with certainty and control, I suppose, wanting no more surprises.

My parents and my aunty were both being called as witnesses and I'd asked my best friend and my IDAS support to be with me on the day. My best friend kept reminding me, 'Focus on what you need, everyone else will sort themselves out, stop worrying about everyone else'. It was very good advice, but I think worrying about others was a distraction from having to think about how I felt, and I was petrified (again).

I drove there with my parents and my aunty and agreed to meet my best friend at the court, as she was coming from the other side of Birmingham. We arrived on the day (emotional and weary), I hadn't slept well the night before, although we'd all commented on how remarkably peaceful the morning had felt. There was a stillness to it, like when you get up early on a summers day but the day hasn't really started properly, like peeking behind the scenes of your favourite play. The promise of something was in the air, justice perhaps, or the quiet before the storm, either way it had an eerie and unexpected calmness to it.

When we arrived at the court, we entered through the 'secret entrance', which isn't so secret, it's just not the main door so you don't have to worry about bumping into the accused. We were ushered to our private room with crap tea and coffee and board games from the 70s and introduced to our volunteer helper. Another friend from school was already there. She had agreed to be a witness as she was the first person I had told. This is a friend I hadn't seen or spoken with (except for Facebook) for many years. I'm so grateful to them for giving me their time and support in this process.

And then there was more waiting. My new favourite hobby (not). I'd like to say it was easy and peaceful, like the volunteers at the court told me it would be, but the truth was for me it wasn't. People were coming in and out constantly to check if we needed anything and to update us on pretty much nothing, as it were. But I think it made people feel helpful to be able to pop in and say things like, 'We're just waiting on a few admin bits before we get kicked off, you'll be on first, Jennifer, can I get you any more tea?'

I was on tenterhooks, shaking, crying, gulping as much Rescue Remedy and inhaling as much frankincense as I could cope with to settle my nerves without getting on a natural high. I was trying to keep all my emotions down, but they kept rising up like unwelcome vomit.

We'd been told the running order for witnesses would start with me, then my family and then my college friend. Each person would be examined by the Crown first (CPS) and then the defence would have their chance to cross-examine. Once the witnesses called by CPS were complete, it would be the turn of defence to put forward their case with their witnesses and the accused. Assuming we started on time, I would have been needed only for the one day. I had planned an evening with my two closest friends, uncertain about what state I'd be in but knowing the right combination of conversation, hugs and prosecco would make it all feel right again.

We were still waiting to get going at lunchtime. I think we all knew something wasn't right, but nobody was talking about the elephant in the room. We tried to make small talk and the lady volunteer from the court certainly kept us all amused with her insane talent for getting our names wrong. The police investigator responsible for my case was there and tried to keep us informed when she was able. Fundamentally, they (the police and CPS) want you fresh in the court room in order to protect the evidence and the integrity of the case, so they're careful what they tell you. They don't take any chances that the evidence will be corrupted by you knowing something, which may prove emotionally challenging or disruptive to the court process. We would be told that a key witness for the defence had not turned up. We were all told to take lunch and be back for 1 pm.

More waiting ...

We were told due to the delay that it was most probable that we wouldn't even get beyond interviewing me on this first day so the rest of the witnesses were told to go home and come back the following day. My parents and aunty would stay until I was called to give evidence and I wouldn't see them again until later that day. My IDAS contact and my best friend would sit in the public viewing gallery so they were close by.

It was around 2 pm, we were told the missing witness had been 'dealt with', and we were on. Standing in court would turn out to be the second most traumatic experience of my life.

I had requested special measures, which are available to witnesses. This should have included being allocated a special court room with a screen and private room attached to the court for any breaks. The private room would have its own entrance into court, which would be screened by a curtain pulled up to the witness box. I would only be able to see the judge, the jury and the barristers. It would mean that I wouldn't have to face seeing 'him' while I entered the room. The private room would provide privacy for me should I need a break or get too upset.

When we had arrived that morning, I enquired about the special measures. They'd been ignored/overlooked. We had been allocated a court room without a curtain or private room. I was told that a screen would be put in place. It would turn out to be a wobbly 2x2m presentation screen propped up against the witness stand blocking the view from me to him and him to me only. The rest of the court room would be wide open. It would also mean there was a chance of him seeing me and vice versa as I entered the room, plus anyone sitting in the public viewing gallery. I was not very happy about this.

Walking into the courtroom, I hesitated by the entrance, looking at the usher, praying for her to tell me he had been removed so I could enter in private. She only said, 'It's okay, you can come in now'. I felt stuck there, unable to move for a second and everything seemed to be in slow motion. I decided to look at the witness box only and walked as fast as I was able to get behind the screen. *Where were those bloody special measures?*

Many people had told me that once you get into the witness box time goes really quickly and you feel calm. Neither of those things were true for me. I rattled and quivered the whole way through like a dotty old lady. My hand was trembling so much I couldn't hold the plastic cup still to drink my water. I had been told before to try and address the jury with my answers, but I felt unable to look at anyone other than the barrister talking to me.

The female barrister from CPS was first. She was very considered and calm in her questioning and her questions mainly required only a 'yes/no/that's true/correct' response confirming the facts as laid out in my statement to the police. It would provide the jury the background and details they needed to have a view of my version of events.

I only remember a few emotionally challenging questions, mainly around the actual incident of rape, the sexual detail. I was asked 'Why now after all this time?', and what I thought I might say to a question like this, which of course I'd imagined would be some Oscar-worthy speech along the lines of taking back my power and helping others to recover, came out as a blubbery wreck about the damage it had caused me, how he'd stolen my virginity. I realised at that moment I hadn't been as strong as I thought I was and that, yes, I wasn't over it, I hadn't forgiven him for all that he'd stolen from me in my life. Another tissue was required; the soggy pile in my other hand getting bigger and bigger.

I was on the stand for roughly two hours for my first interview with CPS. I had been told it could be up to four hours in total. The judge decided to call time there and bring me back in the next day for cross-examination. I was bereft. I'd wanted it done and dusted so I could go home, collapse, have a drink with my friends and know that part was over. All that waiting and I'd have more waiting to come.

I'd put so much thought into my outfit for day one as I'd wanted to look professional, credible, honest, genuine, all things I believed I was. I wanted to be taken seriously. I wanted people to see who I was, to see me. I'd worn a black A-line knee length dress (a favourite of mine) with a royal blue jacket. Now I was facing a second day with no outfit to wear and I would be cross-examined. The worst was yet to come and I didn't feel prepared, I didn't have my armour.

Deflated at home, my friends helped me sort out another suitable outfit. We tried to eat pizza and drank some prosecco. I went to bed leaving my friends to catch up and spent another night fighting the covers and my thoughts. By the time my alarm went off I had been awake for some hours. I was so beyond sleep by this point I wondered if I'd ever sleep again.

Unlike the accused, you are given very little preparation prior to being cross-examined. What little I knew had come from IDAS, who had been brilliant. They had been honest and had explained that it would not be an easy ride. I was prepared for character assassination. I was prepared for my evidence to be picked apart, to seed reasonable doubt into the jury's mind about my perspective on events.

The CPS barrister prosecuting the trial had told me that when the cross-examination began I needed to remember the defending barrister was only doing his job because in the UK we have an impartial justice system. That means everyone deserves a fair hearing and trial regardless of what the barristers believe. He was coming for me. I would only have the safety of the witness stand and my own truth to protect me.

Although I had been mildly prepped for the cross-examination, nothing could have prepared me for my reaction to the experience. When CPS had examined me the day before, there were lots of direct questions requiring a yes or no response. It was easier. The opening statement from the defence barrister was literally like a bullet straight between my eyes.

'Miss Potter, I'm not going to beat around the bush here and waste any more of the judge and jury's time. So I put it to you that events didn't actually happen at all as you have told the judge and jury, but in actual fact, this is something you wanted to happen. In fact, I shall be putting it to you that you instigated the whole event and now, years later, still wrecked with guilt, this is your attempt at covering over your shame.'

Holy shit! What the f***? I had instigated it? I had wanted it? At what point did I drop into someone else's trial? Was this really happening? The room was spinning. I couldn't quite take it in. Suddenly I was no longer merely a witness, I was on trial. I had been disarmed.

And that's how it happens. Before the case, if you're a witness you're not allowed to know anything the accused has said in their statement (to protect the integrity of the case) although the accused can see yours. So prior to being cross-examined, all I knew was that he was pleading 'not guilty'. I also knew he had said sex took place and that I'd consented (which was different to what he'd said to my father on the phone when confronted after it happened). I knew nothing of what story he'd cobbled together. On the morning of the trial I was still naïve enough to think he might change his plea to guilty, that he'd find some morsel of compassion and take responsibility for his wrongdoing. But oh no, he had actually decided to lay blame at my door, in fact 100% of it. I felt like I'd been hit by a stun gun, I couldn't take it in. For a moment I felt like my world had fallen apart.

I had, of course, been warned it was going to be tough. I was prepared for that, for difficult questions, perhaps even about my sex life, my character, definitely about the event itself. But to be accused so directly – that was a shock. As the defence barrister proceeded to try and pick apart my evidence in any way he could – dates I'd got wrong, which hand I was using to hold onto my pants, how could I be sure it was my right hand, what was my left hand doing at the time, whether there'd been any bodily bruising – I was also being drip-fed his version of events, his lies. I remained totally focused on the defence barrister like a missile on precision target. 'Stay present,' I kept saying to myself, 'and tell the truth'. As much as I wanted to run out of the room and head for the hills, 'Just be here right now. Tell the truth.'

The questions kept coming and seemed to get worse. Did the accused complete the sexual act? How did you know that the sexual act was finished? How were you able to leave the bed if he was on top of you? Did you have any bruises on your body afterwards? How is it that a man twice your size didn't bruise you if he forced himself on you like you say? You did in fact call him into the bedroom when you heard him going to the bathroom in the night, didn't you? Why were you only wearing pants and a vest to sleep in when you were in someone else's house? Isn't it true that you were hoping for him to come to you in the night?

They just kept coming. I asked for clarification if I wasn't sure about the question, I denied what lies he put forward and I was very clear that, yes, I did feel shame, but not from guilt.

'Yes, I did feel shame, but it was because of what he DID to me, not what I had chosen.'

There were really uncomfortable questions about the act of sex, some of which I hadn't understood and had to ask for further clarification ('Were you aware of any semen in or leaving your vagina after the event?') It was excruciatingly awkward and felt shameful. I felt parts of myself crumbling away: dignity, pride, confidence, strength. Then, thankfully, a small respite as there was a discussion between the barristers and the judge about doctors' notes not being given as evidence by the prosecution. The judge called time for the extra evidence to be put forward and we were sent outside for a break. We were about one hour in at this point. It had felt like a whole day. Time was not evolving as per normal service.

At this point, had I been given the appropriate special measures, I would have had a private room, but sadly I had to wait outside amongst all the people waiting for their own trial or sentencing, the people from the public viewing gallery, which included his support team, and any other stranger who happened to be passing by.

I had a total breakdown. I sobbed and sobbed until I didn't think I would stop. I was shaking, broken, and disbelief was suffocating me. Sounds were coming out of my body I'd never heard before. The tears and sobs came and I couldn't stop them. I kept saying, 'It's awful, it's really awful, I can't believe it, the lies, how can it be my fault?'

I think with hindsight this howling was also part of my healing, perhaps the level of sobbing I hadn't been brave enough to tackle head on before, and now it was tackling me instead.

My support team had been as shocked as I was with the questioning. The IDAS lady said she'd sat in on a lot of trials and never heard the defence lawyer get so close to the line with his questioning. She was also very good at telling me how well I was doing and that I was coming across as authentic and honest. I didn't feel I could go back in. I couldn't survive another hour of that attack.

While we were outside we were told the judge had decided to move on quickly, and so my family would be brought up from the private room to wait outside the court near where we sat as they would be questioned next. We were told we couldn't talk to each other due to the 'protection of evidence'. They would be frog marched past me to sit twenty yards away. As they passed by they would see the mess I had been in and I was sure both my mum and dad would start to cry, unable to help me, unable to come and wrap me up in their arms. We were all in no man's land. Together but apart. Unable to hug or connect. Alone again. It was pretty awful.

We were called back in. A deep breath. I sat down and looked at the defence barrister again. He questioned me for a further fifteen minutes of wrap-up questions. He was pleasant, quick and to the point. It was like a different barrister in front of me. The judge told me I was free to go. I sat staring at him. He would have to say it again for me to take it in. It was over. I was Frank Bruno, battered but braced for round two with Mike Tyson, but this section had felt like we were having afternoon tea in comparison.

I left my family to give their evidence as I was still unable to communicate with them until they'd been released from court. They would all be in and out within fifteen minutes each, much to all of our surprise and delight.

It was over.

I had learnt that there's a level of human resilience that appears when you need it in the most terrifying of experiences, a level of human strength even the strongest of individuals might not imagine they possess. It's there in all of us. You don't need to train for it, you don't need to practise, it just shows up. If you're ever in a position similar to this, have trust and faith in yourself and your own abilities to be you. Remember your job is easy: all you have to do is tell the truth. Then wrap yourself in all the love and support of your friends and family and give yourself permission to let it in to your heart. You will need it.

14. The quiet after the storm

'Life isn't about waiting for the storm to pass, it's about learning to dance in the rain.'

Anon

After the court case there was a weird surreal feeling around me, almost like disbelief. I couldn't work out if I felt any closure, but there was a feeling of finality. It was over. I wasn't prepared to consider a hung jury situation and have to face it all again. It wasn't going to happen. I wouldn't allow it. What I did know for sure was that I felt very happy to be leaving the court building.

I left through the back (secret) door with my friend to meet another friend in the car park. My family were still waiting to give their evidence. The three of us drove to a nearby services and ordered coffee and cake. We needed to be together for a moment and we needed sugar, something to bring us back around from the weird parallel universe we'd just exited. There was a funny flatness to the air around us. Two of us had been in the room, the other hadn't. I felt guarded and protective, I didn't want my other friend to have it all in her head like we did. We all needed to be together for a moment, to just sit. Looking back, I think I was in shock and had it not been for my best friend I probably would have just come straight home and not said a word. What an ordeal for all of us. It needed to be communicated, to be processed, to be spoken, to be shared.

We gave my other friend the highlights, discussed how awful it had been, shared the rubbishness of it. I listened while my friend recounted how she and the IDAS lady had felt the jury had responded to my time in the stand, the nodding heads, the compassionate faces, the blank curious faces. We discussed the horridness of the defence barrister and even managed a small congratulation for how well I'd held it together, how considered I'd been in my responses to him. There was no telling how it had gone, which way it would go. It was his word versus mine.

Like a well organised tag team, best friend number two kindly drove me home to collect an overnight bag before taking me to my parents' so we could all debrief and be together. My brother, sister-in-law and their three children were also there to offer support and distraction. I was feeling numb.

By the time we arrived at my parents' house, they had all given their evidence and were back home already. I was surprised. My young nieces and nephew wouldn't know where we'd all been, which made debriefing difficult. When we did orchestrate grown-up time, there was a weird reluctance to talk and share. We all seemed to keep our experiences high level, skimming over the detail. I'd wanted to know what questions they'd all been asked, what line of enquiry the barristers had taken, whether there was any further inkling about the strategy the defence were taking. It had all seemed relatively straightforward. There was that strange anti-climax feeling again hanging in the room like an uninvited guest.

I asked my sister-in-law if she'd come for a doggy walk with me; I needed some air. When we arrived at the farm track, I let my crazy cocker spaniel off his lead and put my arm through hers. I still felt I needed to feel close to people I loved. As we walked down the track, we noticed a small furry animal walking calmly in between the small gap of our legs; it was my dog, Murphy. This kind of behaviour was unheard of. Murphy is a lively dog and for the majority of a typical walk he's usually half a mile up front zooming around in his doggy freedom, looking for interesting things to chase. Yet here he was like a chaperone, walking so calmly between our legs, the odd head-lift from left to right to check our faces. It was like he knew we needed taking care of. It was a very precious moment.

I would remember a sense of wanting to put the whole experience into a box and never talk about it again. It was done. It was in the past now. I did feel a sense of release from some of the tension I had been feeling around my shoulders and my back.

The rest of the night would pass like a normal evening with the family together. I'd play with the kids, we'd have tea, a bottle of wine would be opened and then it would be bed. It was over. Although we couldn't take it in, there was some relief.

When the next morning found me at roughly 5 am, I had not slept well at all. I felt like I had a court appearance hangover, I wanted to run away, I needed to be on my own, my shame had returned. I guzzled breakfast and headed off home. I'd arrive at home in such a rush only to find I'd left my house keys at my parents and have to do a one-hour return trip to get them. I was teary by this point and I was conscious that some of the emotion from the day before was bubbling in me. I had this feeling I needed to get somewhere private before the volcano erupted.

When I finally got home, I headed straight for a bath and then got into bed for a snooze after having sobbed double the amount of water into my bath. It was a pretty shit day. I felt lousy. Life was still happening all around me, but I felt suspended in limbo land and totally crap. But I was listening to my feelings, honouring them and not fighting it like my old pattern.

I would later find out my best friend had also spent the next two days in bed, feeling ill. She was so affected by being a passenger to the experience of court, of hearing the detail of one of her closest friend's anguish, of sitting next to 'his' support team in the public gallery, soaking up all the energies of the room. She would be depleted. This was something we hadn't been prepared for. She had been there to support me and in doing so she'd depleted her own reserves.

Although I was so immensely relieved my part in the case was over, I knew there was more to come, including the verdict. I tried to be kind and allow the court hangover to seep its way out. I went to my therapist to talk it through and process what I'd experienced.

I don't think you can prepare for what impact such an experience will have on you. On all of you. I don't doubt for a minute that everyone involved, from the police, to my friends, to my family, to the volunteers, to the jury, to the people in public viewing gallery, are affected in some way.

When I was about fifteen years old I had thought I would go on to study law. I had wanted to be a barrister. I had thought it was a really admirable profession, keeping the streets safe, helping victims, doing the right thing. I can honestly say I don't know how barristers manage to do their job. Nor do I know how police investigators manage to do their jobs, and I truly empathise with them.

Learning to be kind to myself was one of the new skills I would be most grateful for at this part of the process. Going easy on myself, remembering and taking note of the enormity of my experience, not trying to underplay or downsize it (because it would only rear its ugly head in other ways if I tried to ignore it). I would ask every day, 'What do I need today to take a step forward toward feeling better?' Also learning to reach out for support, even if it's just to have another body alongside you.

My mum came to stay one night shortly after the case, and all we did was sit side by side and watch TV, and occasionally I'd nestle into her armpit like I was a teenager again despite being in my late 30s. And for those moments, I felt safe and embraced in love.

15. The verdict & the aftermath

'Keep some room in your heart for the unimaginable.'
MARY OLIVER

I was exhausted, but the real tiredness wouldn't kick in for a few weeks. I was bloody relieved my part in the process was over and that I'd hopefully never have to set foot in a courtroom ever again. The trial continued, he would have his say on the stand and then be cross examined, and the witnesses for the defence would be called forward for questioning, which included his brother and the statement from his ex-wife.

I stayed away from the courts. I wanted to know as little as possible. All I hoped was that the prosecuting barrister turned into a terrier when it was my rapist's turn to be cross-examined. I wanted him to experience the terror I had when his lawyer had turned on me.

Friday was judgment day; verdict day.

The jury would be called in and the judge would summarise everything that had been said so they had the whole course of events fresh in their minds. He would offer them some legal advice and then tell them if they decided on a guilty verdict, the evidence to support it needed to be 'beyond all reasonable doubt'; in other words, they needed to be 100% sure. He would accept a unanimous vote only. All of them needed to agree one way or the other.

It was another long day of waiting. I tried to busy myself with a long dog walk, and around the end of the day my parents arrived to wait for the call from the police investigator, who had suggested I not be on my own when she called in case it was bad news. I was expecting the worse and wondering how I would feel having been through the trauma of court if the verdict came back not guilty.

To be honest, I think we were all convinced it would be 'not guilty'. It was his word versus mine. Right up until the point before being cross-examined, I was not attached to any outcome, I just wanted my day in court to be heard and for him to be held accountable for what he'd done. I genuinely believed what would be would be. However, the cross-examination had felt like a trauma in itself and after learning of his lies, that he was trying to throw all the responsibility and blame onto me, offering no compassion whatsoever, I had changed my mind. The warrior princess in me was angry and wanted justice. I wanted the book thrown at him. I wanted a guilty verdict.

We were sat around the dining table in a mist of eerie silence, little being said, awkward silences, cups of tea. I asked my parents, what do you think is going to happen and no one dared to say what they were thinking.

My mobile rang and I felt my heart drop to my tummy. The police-woman explained the jury had deliberated all day and been unable to agree; it was a hung jury. They'd been unable to get a unanimous decision, so they would be released for the weekend to return on Monday to try again. I was weirdly relieved. At least it wasn't not guilty, there was still hope. But also more waiting and the potential for a hung jury on Monday too.

It was a bloody long weekend. I'd been unable to think about anything else but the case and the verdict. My police contact had asked on the Friday what I wanted to do if it was another hung jury. In other words, did I want a retrial, to go through it all again? I didn't want to think about it. To know how awful it had been to go through it the first time could make it worse a second time, but at least I would be better prepared. I wasn't sure I had the strength to go through it all again so I told her I didn't want to have to think about it unless I had to. I would decide later.

Monday came around quickly and it was time for the jury to return to their room and discuss the case hopefully to a conclusion. On the second day of deliberating, the jury were told the judge would accept a majority vote, which I believe is ten or more from the twelve jury members. I'm not sure why or how the judge decides if a majority vote can be accepted over a unanimous one.

I hadn't slept and I couldn't concentrate on anything. I was expecting the jury to take all day again so I decided to drive into town and mosey around the shops, something I never do. I had ants in my pants and I was restless. I needed a distraction. It was 11 am and I'd just parked in town when my phone rang. It was the police. It had taken the jury one hour.

'We got him, Jen. Guilty verdict.'

I couldn't believe it.

Guilty!

Did she say guilty?

Did we win?

What?

Really?

Guilty!

I was so sure it would go the other way. I had been preparing myself for tears, sorrow, grief. And here I was, speechless, stunned, bewildered. Sentencing would happen in two days and he could serve between five and ten years in prison.

Guilty.

There it was in my life. That word 'guilty', which equated to another important word: justice. The justice I'd prayed about before but given it over to the karma police to sort out. Yet here it was in my reality.

Relief.

Joy.

Shock.

Disbelief.

I couldn't take it in. I called my parents. I called my best friend. I called my other best friend. Mainly we all cried on the phone. Tears of joy, tears of release, tears of shock perhaps?

There was a strange anti-climax to the day. It kind of passed in a weird fog of disbelief. I had this feeling I should do something to mark the occasion, but nothing felt appropriate. It would feel wrong to celebrate. A man had gone to prison for doing something wrong to me. I had been involved in that crime. I had been labelled a victim. I didn't feel good about any of that.

Two days later and the sentencing came in. Five years. He was allocated the minimum. He would likely serve only half of it in a prison, the rest would be on bail. I felt disappointed, which was odd for me because I had started the process unattached to any outcome. *He'd been given the minimum for this kind of case. Did that mean he'd been treated lightly?* It didn't feel fair compared to my twenty years of anguish. I focused on it being prison and that he'd been found guilty and I was very grateful for the outcome. It was finally time to move on.

On the evening of his first night in prison, I sat in my bed awake, snuggled into the bedding. Finally I felt safe. I never thought he would come back for me and attack me again (I didn't think he was that stupid), but I did wonder from time to time if he would send someone else to silence me, such was my paranoia. I did wonder if it would happen again, if there would be a third attack in my life (I still do sometimes when I'm feeling restless). When you've been raped, your safety radar gets turned up to some cosmic level. The slightest wind change, the subtlest of taps on a window, a floorboard creaking, everything was noted. Both times I'd been abused I had been asleep in bed, so bedtime always included an extra dash of caution for me, not the relaxing experience it is for most people. Here I was though, sitting in my bed finally feeling some peace, I could relax. I could sleep again.

I thought about him in his cell for the first night, I wondered what his cell would look like, I tried to imagine what I might feel if I was him. My heart started to race in a panicky way, so I stopped. I realised that wasn't helpful for me. I also realised I wasn't him, I wasn't anything like him. I had compassion, empathy, kindness, consideration, integrity, strong values and morals. I never thought about it again.

I gave myself two weeks to be kind, going steady workwise, doing just the minimum to keep things ticking over. I had treatments booked including acupuncture, network chiropractic care, and therapy in order to support myself back out of the physical and emotional stress. There still wasn't much money coming in but I prioritised investing in me and my wellbeing and I borrowed the rest. I attempted to keep up with my daily meditations and go to my yoga class. I tried to just be, but it felt like it always did, no different. No lightness, no freedom, no joy, no elation. I was still me. The dark heavy cloud was still there. Pants!

I wondered if I'd expected some miraculous turnaround in my life to just happen like a key turning in a lock. Here you go, all the love in the world. It's all yours and it's delicious, you can have it now, you can have all those things you've always wanted. Here they are landing in your lap. You're fixed. Healed. Hoorah, go celebrate.

Only I wasn't. A part of me still felt bland, dull, worthless, hopeless, helpless, ruined, damaged bloody goods (and I was exhausted). I thought it would feel different, I thought healing would occur instantly. I started to wonder whether it would at all and how long it would take. I gave myself full permission to cry into the tears I knew were bubbling up from deep within. Some days after I would catch myself getting a waft of the freedom I thought I would feel all the time, but it would just as soon waft away like a breeze as quickly as it floated in.

A few weeks after the trial, I experienced a whole wave of emotions: ecstasy, elation, disbelief, shock, jubilation, sadness, shame, responsibility, guilt, anger, fury, sadness, loneliness, loss, grief.

I wouldn't know it then but peace would breeze in more permanently eventually, it would just take its time, trying itself out in my life part-by-part until I was more free and at peace than I wasn't. Despite all this, I had an immense sense of pride regarding how brave and courageous I had been. I was also ridiculously proud of how able and willing I had been to be vulnerable and know that it was okay. This felt like a massive step forward in life for me, a jump in my personal growth. I wanted to shout about it, such was my pride.

Sadly, it doesn't just end there. Within a month I'd been approached by witness protection who wanted to know what safety measures I wanted in place for when my rapist was allowed out of prison. This wasn't something I had considered, I was not thinking that far ahead, it wasn't on my horizon that I would need to consider my safety. I was only just getting used to having my sleep again.

It made me reflect how tough it must be for victims of domestic abuse, particularly where there are children involved. How do those women go about having a normal life knowing they'll probably have to see their attacker again? Do they ever get to sleep properly again? What do you say to the children? The ripple effect of the abuse spreads.

A few months after that I received a courtesy call to inform me that my rapist was appealing against his sentence, trying to get it reduced. I was angry to begin with. He already had the minimum possible sentence and he wanted to serve even less? And then I realised again that although he was my rapist, he is also a human being. Who wouldn't want to appeal against their conviction and serve less time locked up? It can't be very nice. No one could want to be in prison. I just hope he has the grace to stay away from me.

And then one day some months after the case was concluded, I was walking around town between client meetings, and I noticed it. The cloud had gone. The weighty dark cloud-shaped balloon strapped dragging behind me was gone. It had been dark grey and the rope I'd been unknowingly holding was thick and uncomfortable. But on this day it was gone. It had just disappeared. There was a lightness in my step, I held my head higher, my chest and my heart felt more open, I was finally facing the world as me, the version of me I always was but chose to cover up from the world.

I finally felt content. The peace I had been waiting for had arrived.

16. Finding hope

'Be as fearless as the women whose stories you have applauded.'
HILARY CLINTON

Some months after the case has concluded, I have learnt to be kind to myself, to know it takes time and that whatever I feel, there is no right or wrong; it just is. I am still processing 'stuff' and probably will for a long time more. I feel able to understand myself and my relation to the world, to my experiences and myself better. I continue to have regular acupuncture and therapy when I need it and I am also continuing to explore other therapeutic tools (still curious as to whether there is indeed a quick fix out there). Overall, I feel freer, lighter, empowered, proud, and although I feel sad for all that being a victim of rape has stolen from me in my life to date, I can no longer allow it to hold me back.

I am grateful for the verdict and recognise I am lucky to get a guilty one despite it being a majority, not unanimous – it matters not to me. The judicial system guidelines are that members of the jury must have 100% conviction in their belief. They are guided to decide 'beyond reasonable doubt', so one individual only needs to have a question mark over one piece of evidence that doesn't stack up to not be able to say 'guilty'. It upsets me deeply to think of all those people who go through court and don't get their guilty verdict (two in three if current stats are to be believed). It really is shocking considering that cases are only put forward if the CPS think there is a good chance of getting a conviction.

Ironically, it wouldn't be the guilty verdict that made the biggest difference to me, it would be own journey through therapy and finding all the places I needed to forgive myself, and to return the burden of responsibility metaphorically to my attackers. Finding some compassion for my attackers also helped, although I feel I don't need to offer them forgiveness for me to feel okay, compassion is enough. What's theirs is theirs, and what's mine is mine.

There is still more we can do to empower women and men to step forward and report their abusers. There is more we can do to improve the police process, although it has come a long way since the explosion of the Jimmy Saville case. There is definitely more we can do to improve the court process, particularly to protect and care better for the victims. There is always more we can do to support those we cherish and love who have been affected by rape and abuse, to hold their hand, and gently guide them to knowing they can live a full life, that rape does not have to wreck lives.

I have always believed that as awful as it was to have experienced being raped, it's made me who I am today. I am stronger, braver, wiser, emotionally more sensitive to others, observant, self-aware, reflective, strong. Sure, I still have tough days when I feel I could grieve forever for the parts of my life I'll never have, but I am having another life, a wonderful one for different reasons, and although I didn't consciously choose it to be that way, it's turned out to be a gift.

'Hope' is the thing with feathers
That perches in the soul,
And sings the tune without the words,
And never stops at all.
And sweetest in the gale is heard;
And sore must be the storm
That could abash the little bird
That kept so many warm.
I've heard it in the chilliest land
And on the strangest sea;
Yet, never in extremity,
It asked a crumb of me.

EMILY DICKINSON

17. Therapies that heal

'Happiness is like a butterfly; the more you chase it, the more it will elude you, but if you turn your attention to other things, it will come and sit softly on your shoulder.'

Thoreau

My journey towards peace has not been smooth or straightforward, rather more like a weird rollercoaster making its way through varied terrain. Sometimes I felt like I was in the driving seat, sometimes a passenger, sometimes I was coasting, feet up at the back, and sometimes I was trailing behind clinging on with my fingertips. I would laugh, I would cry, I would get angry, I would panic and sometimes I might even throw up.

There's something about the word 'journey' that probably needs explaining. To journey can imply there might be a destination; a place you arrive at. In this context, it's like chasing the holy grail or the philosopher's stone: a desire to discover, to learn, to grow but, most importantly, to arrive somewhere and be able to say 'Ta-dahhhh! I am here! I am fixed. I am now healed.'

I have learnt in my journey that there is no elusive end point, grand finale, finishing line destination. The journey is what really counts. Throughout my journey another part of me was given space to heal, to flourish, to find peace. The journey is not over, it will never be over because we are always growing and flourishing (if we allow ourselves to do so). It is a lifelong experience.

I'm very grateful I've always lived with a glass half full mentality. Even on the days when I'd be sobbing by my bed, on my knees, asking, pleading, screaming 'Why me?', there was always at least one cell in my body taking charge, settling things down, asking 'What can I do to make this better?' I attribute and thank my parents for this gift and I truly believe it's kept me alive. You see, after hope, I believe resourcefulness is a key stage of healing; in fact, just knowing you have resources already, which basically mean you have 'choices'.

We don't need to go on a course or get a qualification, we just need to ask the right questions of ourselves. It's the first stage in taking back your power when you've been raped: learning that you are never hopeless or helpless. There is always something that can be done, even if it is choosing to do nothing and just be. That's empowering in itself. What follows are the highlights from my journey through therapies that have helped me along the way which may in some way help you signpost what support could be useful for you.

Curiosity and self-development books

Armed with my resourcefulness and glass half full mentality, the first therapy that helped me love myself again was discovering my talent for coaching. I was always fascinated by people and it's what made me a good leader when I started managing people. I would devour self-development and leadership books by the truckload. The more I knew about the mind and how it worked the more I felt I could gain peace. If I could just understand why he did what he did, maybe it would be okay. Was it something in me that caused it or something in him? Check out the resources at the back of the book for a list of books that helped me.

Neuro-linguistic Programming

Amongst this understanding, I discovered NLP (neuro-linguistic programming), a combined approach to communication, personal development and psychotherapy created by Richard Bandler and John Grinder in the 1970s. It revolutionised how we understand the connection between thoughts, feelings and actions. I read book after book, and many years later I would invest in a practitioner qualification.

NLP opened my already half-full mind to what more might be possible and it gave me some great tools to help me focus, stay in the positive when I was feeling blue, and above all it empowered me. It helped me realise that we have a CHOICE about how we feel.

From time to time deeper feelings would consume me. For me it felt like a volcano. I would notice it stirring. I'd start to get snappy with people for no reason (and then have immense guilt), I would cry over seemingly silly things (and of course I was never really crying for the silly things), my pain bubbled up like hot lava waiting to erupt from the fierce momentum that was building. It was charged. Charged with regret, bitterness, anger, fury, a stolen innocence. For most of the time, I would let it out in the quiet safety of my bedroom, usually sobbing, on my knees, hanging on to the bed, screaming quietly for release and I knew I needed something more in my toolkit.

Tony Robbins, *Unleash the Power Within* Experience

Around 1995, a running buddy of mine asked me if I wanted to go to *Unleash The Power Within*, a weekend conference in London. It was a Tony Robbins experience, four days, total immersion in your life, come out the other side a changed person, full of vitality and focus about what you want in life. It would be my first Tony Robbins event. My best friend had been on it and told me I'd love it. It was a life changing weekend for me. 10,000 strangers in a room at London Excel dancing to Two Unlimited and learning to charge their physical energy to create the right 'state', getting clear about goals they wanted in life and what was driving them deep inside. Besides the fire walk we did on the first night (which was pretty awesome, mainly because I was in Tony Robbins' queue and got to stand alongside the guru himself), the Dickens process was life changing for me.

To go through this Dickens process (a powerful process of transformation) means you'll never adopt the victim mentality or any other limiting beliefs ever again. I was carrying around my baggage (well-hidden of course) at the time, but I did feel like a victim deep down. What I took from the weekend was that life happens for you, not to you. You get to choose whether you're a survivor or a victim. And I knew with my glass half full, there was some victim stuff I needed to drop. I would end up going to the States to do another Tony Robbins experience called *Date with Destiny* some years later whilst waiting for the court case. It was like UPW but on super-power and I'd recommend it to anyone wanting to gain perspective and real personal growth in their life. (Americanisms to one side, you learn to love that part too.)

Acupuncture

Not long after UPW, I would get very ill, mainly from overworking in a stressful job and not taking enough care of my emotional and physical needs. I would go to bed one evening with a sore wrist and wake in the morning with rheumatoid arthritis in every joint in my body. I was unable to feed myself the pain was so bad. Frustrated by the lack of effective treatment by the NHS, I would turn to alternative medicine for hope. I would discover acupuncture and it would end up being a key catalyst of my healing.

I could write a whole book on acupuncture, such was my transformation and fascination with how my body responded to it, so a few years later I would choose to study it for four years. Ancient Chinese philosophy embodies the connection between mind, body and spirit, and so it respects that trauma, both physical and emotional, can be embedded in a human being energetically. Acupuncture works to release and smooth out these blockages using very fine needles in acupressure points on the body so the system can run smoothly. Kind of like giving a car a full MOT.

I was very lucky to have been allocated a lovely practitioner who was not only a brilliant acupuncturist but he was fantastic at holding a therapeutic space for me to just be. No judgement, no mothering or fathering, just a safe space to talk if I wanted to. As I started to recover and trust was established, I started to open like a flower bud in spring. I felt I could talk to him about my life experiences which I knew by this time were holding me back.

I felt so successful at everything I put my hand to, but the one thing I just didn't seem able to achieve was a loving relationship. I'm guessing that he saw the signs early on, but he allowed me to share in my own time. The combination of being able to talk and then having treatment, which was not only smoothing my energy where it was fraught (IBS, headaches, stress, tension in my shoulders from repressed anger, PMT, emotional mood swings, genital traumatic pain), it was releasing some of my trauma too.

A few years later, it would be my acupuncturist who would eventually be the catalyst for me finding a good therapist and making a commitment to that journey. I have a lot to be grateful for from this one man, and I know he will think he was merely doing his job. It was after one of my treatments I realised I had some anger towards my parents which prompted me to investigate the next therapy I tried.

Cognitive behavioural therapy

CBT is a talking therapy (an action oriented psychosocial therapy) that can help you manage your problems by changing the way you think and behave. I liked CBT, it was interesting and it was different. As I sat in one chair having a conversation with my six-year-old self in another, we learnt that the six-year-old was angry because she had been left, abandoned by her parents. I had no idea I felt like this. I felt guilty too, because I saw it through my parents' eyes. What had they been supposed to do? The session enabled me to identify and forgive them by knowing that although I felt that they'd let me down, I also knew that they had done the best they could with what resources they had available to them at the time and that they loved me. It was powerful stuff.

Block clearance therapy

Block clearance therapy was another wonderful explorative therapy for me. It's a process of exploring the soul's journey and any negative associations being held in the subconscious mind. I went to block clearance not long after CBT helped me take the lid off Pandora's box and I wanted to go in and do some further spring cleaning. I'm almost certain I couldn't do it justice to try and explain it, but essentially it allowed me to connect with my younger selves again (similar to CBT) and release what needed to be released. In the visualisations, I mostly remember being aware that a part of me (much younger self) was hiding under a table in a dark cellar, like she didn't want to be seen. She was frightened that bad things would happen. She was playing small, trying not to be noticed. Another WOW moment. That's how I was showing up in life, only giving half of me.

Gratitude

Learning to be grateful is a daily practice that I now embrace and recommend. There is always something to be grateful for and gratitude has the ability to spread your heart. It's expanding rather than contracting like worry and anxiety. Seeing the beauty in simple everyday things like the sunshine, or the smell of wet grass, my nieces and nephews tearing around the house laughing, lovely food, a healthy body, red robins ... whatever brings a smile to your face, gratitude and learning to be okay within myself were two important therapeutic tools that have helped me toward healing.

Most of my coaching clients love the exercise of starting a gratitude journal and writing down all the things they're grateful for each day. They always report a greater sense of wellbeing after just a few days of doing it.

Brené Brown books

This lady deserves another special mention from me. Brené Brown is a research professor who has spent thirteen years studying vulnerability, courage, worthiness and shame, all key themes for those who have been abused. Books have played a major part in my journey as I'm officially a bookaholic, I love learning, I love being curious about the world. In fact, I'm writing this book because I kept looking for a book like this and couldn't find it, but I did find lots of other amazing books that have helped me on my journey. Brené Brown's books in particular. I hold her book *Daring Greatly* like treasure in my heart. It is partly responsible for me daring to walk into the police station to report the rape and also for starting my process of therapy. She showed me what I'd always known but denied about myself, that to be vulnerable is the bravest thing we can choose.

Her books are life changing and well worth the investment.

Exercise and yoga

Dislike of your body is very common after abuse. It's a way of showing dislike to yourself. For many years I would abuse my body in small ways: drunken and stressed smoking, binge drinking, eating the wrong things or too much, hammering my body at the gym, not sleeping enough, not resting enough. I've learnt that it's mainly shame, a disassociation from my body so I can blame it for what happened to me.

Yoga was the first activity which helped me to connect with my body. I have done yoga on and off for fifteen years. What's great about yoga is that it connects you to the moment, it stills you and it draws you into your body. The breathing techniques alone are great for helping you feel grounded, connected and out of your head.

Being able to stand in the mirror and look at myself naked and celebrate the process has taken time, but I now make sure every day I spend time connecting to my body, whether that's taking extra time to put body lotion on after the shower or just noticing myself and telling myself how grateful I am for my beautiful body and my beautiful face. It may sound daft but it makes a massive difference to how we show up if we learn to love and accept ourselves as we are. I've also noticed that I'm glowing more, leaner, slimmer, carrying myself differently as a result. And I've been on no crazy diets or exercise routines, I've just been kinder to myself.

Fun (and cheap) stuff

Connection to joyful activities is another good therapy (and yes, it is a therapy) and it's pretty low cost. I spent time thinking about all the things I love, the activities that bring joy to my life and came up with a list which included dancing, singing, gardening, being in nature, cooking, being with dogs, being with my family, especially little people. I made a small and loose plan to bring more of that into my life. I've been on a flamenco dancing course, singing more than I ever did, discovered five rhythms dance classes, cooked more, spent more time with my family and finally taken the plunge to get my own dog. All these activities bring joy to my life daily; they lift my spirits and they make my soul happy.

Meditation

I would have a love/hate relationship with meditation over the years of healing, but meditation is no longer a bohemian experience kept only for hippies. Steve Jobs, CEO of Apple, swore his daily meditations were responsible for some of his most creative ideas. Brain science now shows that those people who meditate regularly are something like 300% less likely to develop Alzheimer's and dementia due to the fact that new neural pathways are created in your brain while meditating. In other words, your brain is healing.

I so desperately knew it would benefit me (such was my busy mind), but I never seemed able to 'get it'. I'd hear those elusive words 'just clear your mind of all thoughts' and want to charge at the tutor screaming, 'BUT HOW? Have you been inside my head? It doesn't do quiet!' I would keep trying and eventually give up until last year a friend introduced me to Effortless Meditation. I balked at the name, as if any form of meditation could be effortless, but I signed up for the one-day course with Effortless Jo and I never looked back.

It really was effortless, no longer did I need to fight with my mind's chatter, I could embrace it and use it to drop into meditation. It would prove to be a really helpful tool for surviving the stress and anxiety of the court case and I could probably write another book on all the benefits and wonderful adventures I've been on whilst in meditation.

Gestalt therapy

I've written a lot about my recent journey through therapy already and I truly hold it responsible for helping me to learn to love myself, to love my body, to show up as all of me (without hiding any parts of me) and to be able to receive love and be open to the type of relationship I have always dreamt of.

Gestalt is an existential humanistic approach to understanding what it is to be human, especially in relation to others, and it honours the concept of the whole, that we don't get meaning from breaking down into parts but from the appreciation of the whole. I specifically chose gestalt because I understood it would take me out of my head, out of my thoughts. I wanted to connect to my deeper self, to what was lurking in my body, the tension I felt in my chest I knew to be emotional stress, the pain I experienced in my genital area from time to time that I knew was trauma.

I knew I needed to connect, accept, make friends with and gain the wisdom it was trying to give me in order to release, and gestalt did this for me beautifully. It wasn't always easy, in fact some of the sessions I would leave crawling rather than skipping. But it has been fundamental to my learning to be me again, and for that I always hold a very special place in my heart for my therapist.

Havening

A new tool perhaps only three years old born from the research of Professor Ron Ruden. It was discovered that the havening process had the ability to change the brain and detraumatise memories, permanently deleting negative associations to those memories which affect our psyche and our body. It is a gentle process that involves stroking the arms and parts of the face, which thus communicate via neurons to the brain, particularly the amygdala part. When I was having panic attacks in the run-up to the court case, havening would be the tool that would help me stay calm. I could still think that I was frightened and know I was experiencing fear, but my body no longer reacted to ridiculous levels. I was calmer, more thoughtful.

Other therapies

I tried lots of other wonderful therapies along the way, including EMDR, EFT, reiki, reflexology, Access Consciousness, Psych-K, Network Chiropractic Care, all of which have helped me in some way, and I found simple things like reconnecting to my love of dancing and singing, walking the dog in nature, five rhythms dancing, yoga and diet also helpful.

I've been on a mission to try what I can in order to feel whole again. I don't expect others to try as many therapies as I did, but I do gently encourage people who have been through similar events to try something, to notice what appeals to them, what makes them feel light as they explore the different tools out there. To get a recommendation and just try something.

If it doesn't work for you, then try something else. We're all different and there's a myriad of support teams with different tools and techniques to help us all. I learnt to look beyond the obvious, beyond the traditional, to be open minded and willing to try.

Learning to just be 'me' was a critical component, that required me to accept myself as I am. I had to realise that I was trying too hard to 'fix' me because deep down I didn't believe I was enough, I felt I was damaged goods. So if I could just make myself perfect, have the perfect body, the perfect mind, the perfect career, the perfect me ... Of course perfect doesn't exist and actually there is more beauty in accepting ourselves for who we are, for all the good and the bad. So these days I make sure I tell myself every day that I am 'more than enough just as I am'.

18. Getting help

'Onwards to glory.'
JENNIFER POTTER

This chapter could be another book in itself, so I've tried to break it down into sections which consider the different places a person might find themselves in if they are on this journey. At the end of the chapter there is also a list of resources to get more help.

The most important message here is that there is help out there. Find the courage for you or someone you care about to step into the arena and receive help. It will fill up your souls and guide you to where you need to be on your own journey.

If you were abused or raped and hardly anyone knows

Please tell someone, anyone, just someone. Please find someone to talk to. Talking is the first step in allowing all that 'shit' to be released, and this is what needs to happen if you're wanting to start to heal. If you're not ready for the police and the courts, that's fine. You may never be and that's also okay. Just tell someone. If you don't have any one close, then ask for counselling support or approach an organisation like Rape Crisis or IDAS for independent advice.

What if it happened a long time ago?

I didn't report my cases until nearly twenty years after the last incident and look where it got me: to court and a guilty verdict. There is always hope. We just don't know what is possible unless we step forward. And remember, reporting it in itself will help you feel like you're taking some of your power back. It's a virtual nod toward your attacker to say *What you did to me was wrong and I no longer accept that'*.

If you're feeling wobbly/emotional/broken/unworthy/unloved/angry (or any other emotion which is doing your head in)

Please consider finding a good therapist or acupuncturist. My advice here is to find someone you click with. Have a meeting with them, try a session out, see what rapport you get. If you feel like there is a genuine connection betweem you and that they could hold a space for you to explore yourself and your journey, go for it. Know that you can change your mind at any time.

My other advice: be committed to it. You'll probably want a quick fix (like me) and this is a journey, so allow yourself to unfold at the pace you need to. Maybe it will be a quick fix for some of you and maybe it will be longer. There is no right or wrong,

Don't know where to start?

Contact organisations like IDAS, Mind and Rape Crisis. Ask your doctor to recommend local organisations like this; they should know. If they don't, hit the Internet. These organisations are a great support and can help you with whatever decision you make and maybe even help you make a decision that's right for you. There is no right or wrong decision, only what you feel at the time. You are in control.

I'm a parent of someone who's been abused/raped

You need to be brave and patient. My parents didn't have any resources to support them at the time the two incidents happened to me, but now there are lots of things you can do.

To begin with, NO JUDGEMENTS. What's happened has happened, it can't be changed. Your child needs your unconditional love more than ever before. Try to be as open and honest as you can and remember that they don't need to be dealing with your emotional response as well as their own. Sit alongside them, hold their hand, offer hugs and love as much as you can and they're willing to accept. Seek permission to be inside their trauma, My favourite phrase of support is 'What do you need from me right now?' or 'What will help make it better?'

Outside of this, please seek support from IDAS, Rape Crisis, your doctor, a therapist, the internet. I wish my parents had guided me to therapy (and they do too), so gently guide your precious child to professional support but let them feel like they're in control.

I'm a boyfriend/girlfriend/partner of someone who's been abused/raped

They will need your support to learn to love themselves again. Go gently and kindly and allow them to open to you emotionally and physically when they're ready. Ask them questions and be curious. The boyfriends I had who didn't say anything encouraged my self-doubt to kick in, assuming they were planning their exit strategy from me because I was damaged goods. Try to be non-judgemental and know that it's hard for us to talk sometimes, but with your support, love and encouragement we can know our beauty again from the inside out.

Learn to be open to receiving and asking for help

I feel that I was pretty brave in my journey, going to the police by myself, being interviewed alone, but what I later learnt was that this was just my inability to ask for help. If you're about to tell the police or in the middle of the process, please get some support. Reach out to friends and ask them to come and sit with you. Don't be alone in this. Even if you don't want to talk about it, just having support and comfort will be beneficial to you. Try and put yourself in a space where you're open to receiving (but feel safe of course). Learn how to ask for help, and if someone can't, try not to take it personally. It doesn't mean they don't want to, they just can't. So keep on asking until you find someone who can.

Getting peace amongst the 'shit'

If you haven't discovered the modern benefits of meditation, it's definitely worth trying. Mindfulness and meditation are really gaining support in this modern information-overloaded world and I have found it to be massively helpful for me. I would recommend Effortless Meditation courses by Effortless Jo. She travels the UK doing courses. Even my mum and dad (a tough Yorkshire bloke with a big heart) took to it after I started and they practise more than I do now.

Whatever you decide, know this: you are a precious, wonderful human being and you deserve all that life has to offer you. Nobody gets to take that away from you. Use your experiences to empower you to choose the life you want and shine your light with freedom!

Please also check out the resources pages at the back of the book.

Afterword

It's been twelve months since the court case. Life has continued to unfold kindly for me, I'm pleased to say. It hasn't been a totally easy year, but then life isn't smooth, is it? The downs definitely help us to appreciate the ups, and I'm pleased to say there have been fewer downs than I've had in previous years.

The summer came and went. I mindfully approached it wondering if the same 'dip' I'd come to know so well in previous years would show itself as strongly as the anniversary of the rape circled back around. I'm pleased to report that although the dip did happen, it was significantly less charged than previous years. Long may it continue, and here's hoping every year it gets less and less.

I pushed on writing this book, which remarkably came out of me relatively easily in only six weeks. Deciding what to call it, how to get it published and actually getting it into the world was less easy. The writing process was really cathartic and I'd encourage everyone who's had or is having a tough time to put pen to paper and let the words flow. I didn't write the first draft in chronological order, so when I put it together and read it through for the first time from start to finish, it was really interesting to see which bits in the journey I'd missed out. I noticed I had lightly touched on the rape incident (fearing judgement of others) and completely skipped over the moment I told my parents. This was a powerful part in the process for me. I think on some level I was trying to protect my parents; I didn't want them to be judged by their actions either.

When I sat down to finally write the missing piece about my disclosure to my parents I had the realisation that the isolation and loneliness I'd experienced from feeling unlovable was created by me in that moment. I had decided that my parents wouldn't be able to love me anymore and if they couldn't love me why would anyone else. I'd trapped myself in a bubble of never to be loved. It had been my choice. And boom, there it was: permission to feel lovable again. It was after this moment I really started to unfold in my journey of learning to love myself again, reading more books, attending more courses – yep, that lesson about just being, slowing down and appreciating 'what is' still needs some further work! Perhaps I should just embrace the seeker in me?

With the book almost finished and ready to put out to the world, I shrank small again. I was feeling stuck with it. It was just before Christmas and I sensed I wasn't ready to put my story out there. I was still tired, physically, mentally and emotionally drained. The court case really took a lot out of me and with hindsight I really didn't give myself enough time and space to heal from it. I was still building my business and getting money in was tough, which meant holidays were a struggle financially. I wish with hindsight that I'd begged, borrowed, found a way to get a proper two-week break from everything and that I'd had it planned for just after the court case. I intend to fix that this year with way more holidays and rest.

Many people ask how my parents are doing and I'm pleased to say they're doing really well. The experience of going through the process of reporting the incident has brought us closer together, we're more open and honest, more understanding with each other. We value our time with each other and I think we all sense a greater level of freedom as a result of the court case conclusion. I sense it's liberated us from each other in a healthy way, taken away some of the guilt, the shame, resettled responsibilties. I feel it really took its toll on my dad and I know a part of him still feels in some way that he let me down and that he should have protected me somehow at the time or after. We talk about it (sometimes). I reassure him there was nothing he could have done, and when talk turns to the 'beating' that could have taken place, I'm grateful that it didn't because I'd rather have my dad alongside me than in prison for actual bodily harm. Sexual violence affects those that love you too, they have their own emotions to process.

Just before Christmas I had the opportunity to share my story on stage. It was a small and intimate gathering of about 200 people. I would be teeing up the keynote speaker, Meirion Jones, who was the lead investigative journalist responsible for breaking the Jimmy Saville scandal. It felt like the universe had created this opportunity for me to test how it felt speaking in public about my journey.

I have spoken on stage to audiences of over 500 people, but this was different. It would be my story. I made a deal with the universe in the car on the way over to Manchester: 'If this goes well and it feels good to share my story, I'll do more. If it or I flop, it's over, I choose a different path.' Well, despite my unusual level of nerves, it would turn out to be a precious and special moment for me. I've never felt so contained, so calm on stage. I felt powerful and vulnerable, steady and emotional, clear and compassionate. And so a deal was won by the universe and I decided to crack on with getting this book out to the world. I felt a strong connection to a purpose to help others.

Christmas came with a gift of a virus and I was finally grounded for a week in the house, just me and Murphy dog (with the odd soup-delivering visitor). I had been advised to write a blog to support the book launch and decided to crack on with that whilst I was glued to my sofa and back-to-back episodes of *Game of Thrones*. I started to dread the thought I would need a name (the book was still known as 'the book with no name') and yet within an hour of playing with my new blog, I had discovered the name *Brave Souls*.

After the months of to-ing and fro-ing over a book name, the blog didn't take any effort at all. It felt right, it was all finally coming together. I hoped the book and the blog would act as a call to arms for those brave souls trying to find their tribe, to know they were not alone.

Early in 2016, I had my first comment from a fellow brave soul waiting for her court case. She'd found my blog. She sent me such a wonderful note. I sat in my bed one morning reading it and weeping. They were happy tears. Something really positive had come from something really shite.

In the end it wasn't the guilty verdict that made the biggest difference to me, and in fact I'm left wondering whether prison will really help my rapist to rehabilitate or not. The guilty verdict was indeed the cherry on the cake and it did go some way to nudging closure closer. What mattered more was that I spoke out, that I chose to say that what happened to me was wrong. And even more important than that was that I turned the lens back on myself and started to focus on my own wellbeing, my happiness and my healing through therapy and acupuncture.

I spend a lot of time wondering if I can reach the point of total forgiveness. All the spiritual development books I read seem to indicate this as being the key to total healing. I no longer have any serious charge of emotion for my rapist and some days I actually feel empathy towards him. On other days, the grief of what I've lost, the opportunities I've missed overwhelm and suffocate me and I give myself permission to have a cry until I can cry no more. These moments are getting fewer and fewer and there are fewer tears. I hope at some point I will come to total forgiveness. In fact, I'm sure I will. For now, forgiveness of myself will be sufficient.

In writing and publishing this book I hope I can help many others to heal and to thrive. To get their lives back like I have.

With much love and hope for your own healing, Jennifer x

Acknowledgements

My gratitude knows no bounds for all the wonderful people who've not only helped me along my journey at some point or another, but also to those individuals who've been significant in helping me craft, write and publish this book.

I'm so lucky to have such big hearted and open-minded parents who have always encouraged me to dare greatly, believe in the impossible and make my dreams come true. They have stood alongside me in my journey and through court with total dedication, love and support, despite their own pain. They encouraged me to write and publish this book even though I feared 'putting it out there' toward the end, it was their gentle nudge that made me believe it would be a good thing to do for me and for other BraveSouls.

To my best friends, Nicola and Laura, my love for you is bottomless. Thank you for keeping me sane, for being my guardian angels, for reminding me I have a sense of humour and being by my side through all the ups and downs in life, I'm a lucky lady to have your love and support.

Special thanks to the book's 'godparents', Jo and Brian, thank you, thank you, thank you. This book would be sitting on my hard drive were it not for your consistent support, gentle encouragement and honest feedback through my wobbles, especially when I was scared to pop my head above the parapet.

To all the wonderful therapists and practitioners who've inspired, cared and opened my heart again. With very special thanks to Tom, Christine and Alex. What a gift you all have to share with the world.

For Sam at IDAS charity for helping me to see that my journey to letting go required me to write this 'damn book' in the first place and for being able to hold my hand through such a traumatic experience, you're a soul sister for life.

Thanks also to all the other characters along the judicial journey, from the amazingly supportive and encouraging police women, especially Julie for believing me so wholeheartedly.

Special thanks also to my fab book support group for editing (Gary, Kyla & Judith), reviewing (all the early readers), creating (Ned & Rob), spreading the word and for reminding me to be proud of what I'm trying to do. Feeling like I had a team behind me, really kept me going.

And for any wonderful friends, colleagues, acquaintances that have ever wiped my tears, held my hand, encouraged me to laugh and believe in what's possible, my love and gratitude to you always.

And finally a massive and heart warming thankyou for everyone who donated to my crowd funding campaign to help me get this book published and birthed into the world in a way that would help me to serve those that need this book. It's because of you this book can now go do some good for other Brave Souls.

Much gratitude and love to you all x

Other helpful resources:

Rape Support Organisations

Rape Crisis – www.rapecrisis.org.uk

Sexual Assault Referral Centres – To find your nearest one, go to the NHS site and search for SARC http://www.nhs.uk/Service-Search/ Rape-and-sexual-assault-referral-centres/LocationSearch/364

IDAS - Example of a local charity supporting women and men through recovery, disclosure and court proceedings, and also the charity that supported me https://www.idas.org.uk

Support specifically for men & boys

Mankind - http://www.mankindcounselling.org.uk

National Association for People Abused in Childhood - http://na-pac.org.uk

Therapy and holistic therapies that support the healing journey

- **Acupuncture** – Visit The British Acupuncture Council page and search for a registered practitioner near you http://www.acupuncture.org.uk

- **Gestalt Therapy** – Sadly, there isn't one directory to find these people. I did a Google search for 'gestalt therapist' + the name of my local town/city. You also could try one of these as a starting point. 0-4op or http://gestaltcentre.org.uk The key here is to find someone you can work with. So notice who you are drawn to and ask to meet them before deciding if you want to work with them or not.
- **Block Clearance Therapy** – **http://www.blockclearance.com**
- **Havening** – http://www.havening.org
- **Cognitive behavioural therapy** – Visit the lead organisation for CBT in the UK http://www.babcp.com
- **NLP** – To find a practitioner who is NLP trained, Google 'NLP' + 'coach' or 'practitioner'. To do some training in NLP, Google 'NLP+practitioner training'.
- **Meditation** – There are many meditation classess now available, but I would only recommend http://www.wearebrave-souls.co.uk because it's who I learnt with. She offers one-day group workshops around the UK and also 121 learning.

There are of course many more wonderful therapies that help, from reflexology to reiki to network chiropractic care to Psych-K and Access Consciousness. The trick is finding one that appeals, finding a practitioner you can talk to and giving it a go. It most likely will lead you on to other therapies. It's a journey not a destination.

Books and other resources that helped me

- Brené Brown – All of her books helped me in some way, but particularly Daring Greatly and The Gifts of Imperfection. Check them out here http://brenebrown.com
- Clarissa Pinkola Estes – Women Who Run with the Wolves is a fantastic book about reclaiming your feminine psyche and should be on every woman's bookshelf http://www.clarissapinkolaestes.com
- Dr Nina Burrowes books – Fantastic for recovery from trauma for the individual, parents and support team. http://ninaburrowes.com She also specialises in training juries, judges and barristers.
- Vivian Broughton for deeper understanding of trauma. http://www.vivianbroughton.com Go to resources and books. Two that helped me were Becoming your True Self and The Heart of Things.
- Martha Beck – Another fine writer. Anything of hers, but particularly Finding your North Star and Finding Your Way in a Wild New World. http://marthabeck.com
- Caroline Myss – Anatomy of the Spirit book
- Tony Robbins – Unleash the Power Within book.
- Dain Heer – Being you, Changing the World book. Something a little different, but a powerful book that will set you free from judgement if you can keep an open mind.
- Marianne Williamson – A Return to love
- Dr Mark Epstein – Going to Pieces Without Falling Apart
- Alison Armstrong – The Queen's Code
- Lisa Lister – Code Red and Love Your Lady Parts

Gurus and inspirational people worth a follow on social media

Brené Brown

Martha Beck

Elizabeth Gilbert

Tony Robbins

Lisa Lister

Clarissa Pinkola Estes

Wayne Dyer

Keeping in touch

I'm not sure yet where this book will take me, but I do know that I hope to help inspire other people like me to start to heal from their trauma and to be able to speak about their abuse. If you want to reach out or find out more about what next, you can find me at www.wearebravesouls.co.uk , in the facebook group facebook.com/wearebravesouls and on instagram @jensbravesoul